2024 Easy

Keto Diet

Book for Beginners

Over 60

1900 Days of Quick, Low Sugar & Low Carb Keto Recipes Cookbook

to Help Shed Extra Fat | Incl. Friendly 30 Day Meal Plans

Astrid D. Mathiesen

Warning and Disclaimer:

The content presented in this work is provided for educational and entertainment purposes only. While every effort has been made to ensure its accuracy and reliability, no warranties, express or implied, are provided. The author does not offer legal, financial, medical, or professional advice. By accessing this material, the reader acknowledges that the author and publisher are not liable for any direct or indirect losses resulting from the utilization of the information presented herein, including but not limited to errors or omissions.

Furthermore, readers are advised to exercise caution and discretion when applying the concepts discussed in this work to their personal or professional lives. It is recommended to seek guidance from appropriate experts or professionals before making significant decisions based on the contents herein. The author and publisher disclaim any responsibility for any unfavorable outcomes arising from the application of the ideas, recommendations, or strategies outlined in this work.

Table of Contents

Introduction

As a passionate nutritionist and culinary explorer, my deep dive into the world of diets has unveiled the incredible benefits of the ketogenic lifestyle. After thorough research and personal experience, I've discovered that the ketogenic diet stands as a beacon of health and efficiency, promoting fat as the primary fuel source instead of glucose. This metabolic shift, known as ketosis, unlocks numerous health advantages, including weight loss, improved blood sugar levels, and increased energy.

Transitioning to a keto diet, however, can be daunting. Finding delicious, fulfilling meals that adhere to keto principles is a common challenge. This is precisely where this cookbook shines. I have meticulously curated an array of recipes that not only align with keto guidelines but also excite the palate. Whether you are a newcomer to keto, a seasoned follower, or simply looking to spice up your low-carb regimen, this cookbook is your go-to guide.

Inside, you'll uncover a treasure chest of delectable recipes for every meal of the day. From nourishing breakfasts and lively lunches to indulgent dinners and decadent desserts, each recipe is designed to make your keto journey enjoyable and sustainable. Say farewell to the dull routine of repetitive meals and welcome a world of culinary creativity that will make carb cravings a thing of the past.

Recognizing that starting a new dietary journey can be overwhelming, this cookbook also provides essential knowledge and practical tips for keto success. Discover which foods to embrace and which to avoid, master keto-friendly cooking techniques, and learn effective strategies for meal planning and portion control.

This cookbook is more than just a collection of recipes—it's an invitation to a healthier lifestyle. It's about experiencing joy and satisfaction in your diet while striving toward your wellness goals. The insights, tools, and inspiration found within these pages will empower you to confidently navigate the ketogenic lifestyle.

Whether you're a dedicated keto devotee or just embarking on this transformative path, we invite you to explore the vast possibilities this cookbook offers. Get ready to enjoy mouthwatering dishes, rejuvenate your health, and experience the remarkable benefits of the ketogenic diet. Embrace this opportunity to nourish your body and mind, and set forth on a culinary journey that promises to bring vitality and vibrancy to your life.

Your Comprehensive Guide to the Ketogenic Diet

What is the Keto Diet?

The ketogenic diet, commonly referred to as the keto diet, is a low-carbohydrate, high-fat dietary plan designed to transform your body's primary fuel source from carbohydrates to fats. This shift aims to induce a metabolic state called ketosis, where your body relies on ketones, produced from the breakdown of fats, as its main energy source.

The Science Behind the Keto Diet

Under normal dietary conditions, carbohydrates are converted into glucose, which is the body's primary energy source. When you significantly reduce your carbohydrate intake and increase fat consumption, your body's glucose reserves become depleted. This triggers the liver to start converting stored fats into ketones, which then serve as the primary energy source for both your body and brain.

Key Principles of the Keto Diet

Carbohydrate Restriction: Limit your carbohydrate intake to about 20-50 grams per day, which constitutes roughly 5-10% of your total daily calories. This restriction is essential to enter and maintain ketosis.

High Fat Intake: Increase your consumption of healthy fats, making up about 70-80% of your daily calorie intake.

Moderate Protein: Consume moderate amounts of protein, typically 20-25% of your daily calories, from sources like meat, poultry, fish, and eggs.

Daily Intake Guidelines

Carbohydrates: 20-50 grams per day

Fats: 70-80% of daily calories

Protein: 20-25% of daily calories

Primary Food Choices

High-Quality Fats: Avocados, nuts, seeds, olive oil, coconut oil, butter, and cheese.

Proteins: Meat, poultry, fish, eggs, and plant-based protein sources for vegetarians and vegans.

Low-Carb Vegetables: Leafy greens, broccoli, cauliflower, zucchini, bell peppers, and asparagus.

Benefits of the Keto Diet

Weight Loss: By reducing insulin levels and boosting fat burning, the keto diet can lead to significant weight loss, particularly from stored body fat.

Improved Blood Sugar Control: Enhances insulin sensitivity, beneficial for those with type 2 diabetes or prediabetes.

Increased Energy Levels: Ketones provide a steady and efficient energy source, helping reduce fatigue and boost overall energy.

Enhanced Mental Clarity: A steady supply of ketones to the brain can improve focus, cognitive function, and mental clarity.

Cardiovascular Health: Potential improvements in cholesterol levels (higher HDL and lower triglycerides) and blood pressure.

Getting Started with the Keto Diet

Transitioning to a keto diet can be challenging, but proper understanding and preparation can ease the process. Start by gradually reducing your carbohydrate intake and increasing your consumption of healthy fats and proteins. Track your macronutrient intake to ensure you're meeting the keto guidelines.

Important Considerations

Consultation: Before starting the keto diet, consult with a healthcare professional or a registered dietitian to ensure it's suitable for your individual health needs and to receive personalized guidance.

Whole Foods: Focus on nutrient-dense, whole foods to ensure you're meeting your nutritional needs.

Hydration and Electrolytes: Stay hydrated and consider electrolyte supplements to avoid imbalances during the initial phase of ketosis.

The Advantages of the Keto Diet

The ketogenic diet, known for its low-carb, high-fat approach, offers a myriad of benefits that extend beyond weight loss. Here are some notable advantages of following a well-structured ketogenic diet:

1. Effective Weight Loss

One of the most well-documented benefits of the keto diet is its ability to promote weight loss. By drastically reducing carbohydrate intake and increasing fat consumption, the body enters a state of ketosis, where it burns fat for fuel instead of glucose. This shift not only facilitates significant weight loss but also helps in reducing hunger and controlling cravings, making it easier to maintain a healthy weight over time.

2. Enhanced Energy and Mental Sharpness

Many individuals on the keto diet report experiencing sustained energy levels and improved mental clarity. Ketones, the alternative fuel produced from fats, provide a consistent and efficient energy source for the brain. Unlike the energy swings associated with high-carb diets, the keto diet offers stable energy, enhancing focus, concentration, and cognitive function.

3. Superior Blood Sugar Management

The keto diet is particularly beneficial for those dealing with insulin resistance, prediabetes, or type 2 diabetes. By limiting carbohydrate intake, the diet helps stabilize blood sugar levels and reduces the need for insulin. This improved glycemic control can lower the risk of diabetes-related complications and support overall metabolic health.

4. Reduced Inflammation

Chronic inflammation is a root cause of many health issues, including heart disease and autoimmune disorders. The ketogenic diet has been shown to reduce inflammation markers in the body. Incorporating anti-inflammatory, nutrient-rich foods into a keto diet can further decrease inflammation and enhance general health.

5. Improved Heart Health

Contrary to earlier misconceptions, a well-structured ketogenic diet can support heart health. It can lower triglycerides, raise high-density lipoprotein (HDL) cholesterol, and improve other cardiovascular markers. Emphasizing high-quality fats from sources such as avocados, nuts, seeds, and olive oil is essential for achieving these heart health benefits.

6. Enhanced Metabolic Function

The keto diet positively influences various metabolic markers. It increases insulin sensitivity, which is crucial for maintaining balanced blood sugar levels and preventing insulin resistance. The diet also helps reduce markers of metabolic syndrome, including abdominal fat, blood pressure, and fasting insulin levels, contributing to overall metabolic health and lowering the risk of chronic diseases.

7. Therapeutic Benefits for Specific Conditions

Beyond its general health benefits, the keto diet has shown promise in managing certain medical conditions. It has been extensively used in treating epilepsy, particularly in children, where it can significantly reduce seizure frequency. Preliminary research also indicates potential benefits for neurodegenerative diseases like Alzheimer's and Parkinson's, as well as conditions like polycystic ovary syndrome (PCOS). However, further studies are needed to fully understand these therapeutic applications.

Important Considerations

While the keto diet offers numerous benefits, it may not be suitable for everyone. Individual responses can vary, and it is important to consult with a healthcare professional before starting the diet, especially if you have underlying health conditions. A personalized approach and proper monitoring can ensure that the diet aligns with your specific health needs and goals.

Who Benefits from the Keto Diet?

The ketogenic diet, with its low-carb, high-fat approach, offers a variety of benefits for different groups of individuals. Here's a closer look at who might find the keto diet particularly advantageous:

1. Individuals Struggling with Obesity

For those battling obesity, the keto diet can be an effective weight loss tool. By reducing carbohydrate intake and increasing fat consumption, this diet helps to reduce hunger and increase feelings of fullness. This can lead to a significant reduction in calorie intake, promoting sustained weight loss and making it easier to maintain a healthy weight.

2. People with Type 2 Diabetes

The keto diet can be highly beneficial for individuals with type 2 diabetes. By drastically reducing carbohydrate intake, the diet helps stabilize blood sugar levels and improve insulin sensitivity. This can lead to better glycemic control and potentially reduce the need for diabetes medications.

3. Individuals with Neurological Disorders

The keto diet has shown promising results in managing certain neurological conditions. It has been particularly effective in reducing seizures in epilepsy patients, especially children. Additionally, emerging research suggests potential benefits for neurodegenerative diseases such as Alzheimer's and Parkinson's disease, though more studies are needed to confirm these effects.

4. Women with Polycystic Ovary Syndrome (PCOS)

Women suffering from PCOS may find relief through the keto diet. By improving insulin sensitivity and reducing levels of circulating insulin and androgens, the diet can help manage symptoms associated with PCOS, such as irregular menstrual cycles and weight gain.

5. Endurance Athletes

Endurance athletes may benefit from the keto diet due to its ability to enhance fat utilization. By adapting to a diet high in fats and low in carbs, athletes can improve their stamina and decrease their reliance on glycogen stores, potentially boosting performance during prolonged physical activities.

Important Considerations

While the keto diet offers numerous benefits, it is essential to recognize that it may not be suitable for everyone. Consulting with a healthcare professional before making any significant dietary changes is crucial, particularly for individuals with underlying health conditions.

Who Should Exercise Caution with the Keto Diet?

Certain individuals should approach the keto diet with caution or avoid it altogether:

Individuals with Certain Medical Conditions: Those with liver or pancreatic disease, gallbladder disease, or a history of pancreatitis may find the keto diet unsuitable.

Pregnant or Breastfeeding Women: The keto diet may not provide adequate nutrients for fetal development and could impact milk production.

Individuals with a History of Eating Disorders: The restrictive nature of the keto diet may exacerbate disordered eating patterns.

Individuals with a History of Kidney Stones: The high-fat content of the keto diet might increase the risk of kidney stone formation.

Children: Due to their higher carbohydrate needs for growth and development, the keto diet may not be appropriate for children.

Tips for Successfully Starting the Keto Diet

1. Educate Yourself and Plan Ahead

Before diving into the keto diet, take the time to educate yourself about its principles and benefits. Understanding how the diet works will help you make informed choices. Plan your meals in advance to ensure you're hitting the right macronutrient ratios and getting adequate nutrients. A well-thought-out meal plan can help you stay on track and make the transition smoother.

2. Gradually Reduce Carbs

Instead of cutting out all carbohydrates at once, consider gradually reducing your carb intake over a few weeks. This gradual reduction can help minimize the symptoms of the "keto flu," which include headaches, fatigue, and irritability, making the transition to ketosis easier on your body.

3. Focus on Healthy Fats

While the keto diet is high in fats, it's crucial to prioritize healthy fat sources. Include foods like avocados, olive oil, nuts, seeds, and fatty fish in your diet. These fats provide essential nutrients and support overall health, helping you feel satiated and energized.

4. Stay Hydrated and Balance Electrolytes

Hydration is key on the keto diet. Drinking plenty of water helps prevent dehydration and constipation. Additionally, maintaining proper electrolyte balance is crucial. Consider adding a pinch of salt to your water or consuming electrolyte-rich foods like leafy greens and nuts to avoid electrolyte imbalances.

5. Track Your Progress

Monitoring your ketone levels can help you stay in ketosis and adjust your diet as needed. You can use urine strips, breath analyzers, or blood ketone meters to keep track of your progress. Tracking your ketones helps you understand how your body responds to different foods and can guide your dietary adjustments.

6. Be Prepared for Social Situations

Social events and dining out can be challenging on the keto diet. Plan ahead by researching restaurant menus for keto-friendly options or bringing your own snacks to gatherings. You can also offer to bring a keto-friendly dish to share, ensuring you have something to enjoy while staying on track.

7. Consult with a Healthcare Professional

Before starting the keto diet, it's advisable to consult with a healthcare professional, especially if you have any underlying health conditions. A doctor or dietitian can provide personalized guidance and ensure the diet is appropriate for your individual health needs.

8. Listen to Your Body

Pay attention to how your body responds to the keto diet. Everyone's experience is different, so it's important to listen to your body and adjust accordingly. If you experience persistent adverse effects, it may be necessary to re-evaluate your approach or seek professional advice.

9. Join a Support Community

Having support can make a big difference in your keto journey. Join online communities, forums, or local groups where you can share experiences, get advice, and stay motivated. Support from others who are on the same journey can be invaluable.

Conclusion

Starting the keto diet can be a transformative experience, offering numerous health benefits. By educating yourself, planning ahead, and making mindful choices, you can navigate the challenges and enjoy the rewards of a ketogenic lifestyle. Remember to prioritize nutrient-dense foods, stay hydrated, and seek support when needed to ensure long-term success and well-being.

CHAPTER 1 Breakfast Delights

Mushroom Frittata

Preparation time: 10 minutes | Cook time: 15 minutes | Serves 6

- ✓ 2 tablespoons olive oil
- ✓ 1 cup sliced fresh mushrooms
- ✓ 1 cup shredded spinach
- ✓ 6 bacon slices, cooked and chopped
- ✓ 10 large eggs, beaten
- ✓ ½ cup crumbled goat cheese
- ✓ Sea salt
- ✓ Freshly ground black pepper

Instructions

1. Preheat the oven to 350°F. 2. Place a large ovenproof skillet over medium-high heat and add the olive oil. 3. Sauté the mushrooms until lightly browned, about 3 minutes. 4. Add the spinach and bacon and sauté until the greens are wilted, about 1 minute. 5. Add the eggs and cook, lifting the edges of the frittata with a spatula so uncooked egg flows underneath, for 3 to 4 minutes. 6. Sprinkle the top with the crumbled goat cheese and season lightly with salt and pepper. 7. Bake until set and lightly browned, about 15 minutes. 8. Remove the frittata from the oven, and let it stand for 5 minutes. 9. Cut into 6 wedges and serve immediately.

Per Serving:

calories: 379 | fat: 27g | protein: 16g | carbs: 1g | net carbs: 1g | fiber: 0g

Lemon-Blueberry Muffins

Preparation time: 5 minutes | Cook time: 20 to 25 minutes | Makes 6 muffins

- ✓ 1¼ cups almond flour
- ✓ 3 tablespoons Swerve
- ✓ 1 teaspoon baking powder
- ✓ 2 large eggs
- ✓ 3 tablespoons melted butter
- ✓ 1 tablespoon almond milk
- ✓ 1 tablespoon fresh lemon juice
- ✓ ½ cup fresh blueberries

Instructions

1. Preheat the air fryer to 350°F (177°C). Lightly coat 6 silicone muffin cups with vegetable oil. Set aside. 2. In a large mixing bowl, combine the almond flour, Swerve, and baking soda. Set aside. 3. In a separate small bowl, whisk together the eggs, butter, milk, and lemon juice. Add the egg mixture to the flour mixture and stir until just combined. Fold in the blueberries and let the batter sit for 5 minutes. 4. Spoon the muffin batter into the muffin cups, about two-thirds full. Air fry for 20 to 25 minutes, or until a toothpick inserted into the center of a muffin comes out clean. 5. Remove the basket from the air fryer and let the muffins cool for about 5 minutes before transferring them to a wire rack to cool completely.

Per Serving:

calories: 188 | fat: 15g | protein: 6g | carbs: 7g | net carbs: 5g | fiber: 2g

Almond Flour Pancakes

Preparation time: 5 minutes | Cook time: 10 minutes | Serves 6

- ✓ 2 cups (8 ounces / 227 g) blanched almond flour
- ✓ ¼ cup erythritol
- ✓ 1 tablespoon baking powder
- ✓ ¼ teaspoon sea salt
- ✓ 4 large eggs
- ✓ ⅔ cup unsweetened almond milk
- ✓ ¼ cup avocado oil, plus more for frying
- ✓ 2 teaspoons vanilla extract

Instructions

1. In a blender, combine all ingredients and blend until smooth. Let the batter rest for 5 to 10 minutes. 2. Preheat a large, very lightly oiled skillet over medium-low heat. (Keep oil very minimal for

perfectly round pancakes.) Working in batches, pour circles of batter onto the pan, 2 tablespoons (⅛ cup) at a time for 3-inch pancakes. Cook 1½ to 2 minutes, until bubbles start to form on the edges. Flip and cook another minute or two, until browned on the other side. 3. Repeat with the remaining batter.

Per Serving:

calories: 355 | fat: 31g | protein: 12g | carbs: 12g | net carbs: 5g | fiber: 7g

Coffee Smoothie

Preparation time: 5 minutes | Cook time: 0 minutes | serves 2

- ✓ 1 cup unsweetened hemp milk
- ✓ ½ cup ice
- ✓ ⅓ cup cold-brew coffee
- ✓ ½ avocado
- ✓ 2 tablespoons cacao powder
- ✓ 1 scoop plant-based, low-carb protein powder (such as Truvani or Sunwarrior brands) (optional)
- ✓ 2 or 3 drops liquid stevia

Instructions

1. Combine all the ingredients in a blender and blend on high until creamy and smooth. 2. Divide between tall serving glasses and enjoy chilled.

Per Serving:

calories: 130 | fat: 9g | protein: 3g | carbs: 8g | net carbs: 4g | fiber: 4g

Mini Spinach Quiche

Preparation time: 5 minutes | Cook time: 15 minutes | Serves 1

- ✓ 2 eggs
- ✓ 1 tablespoon heavy cream
- ✓ 1 tablespoon diced green pepper
- ✓ 1 tablespoon diced red onion
- ✓ ¼ cup chopped fresh spinach
- ✓ ½ teaspoon salt
- ✓ ¼ teaspoon pepper
- ✓ 1 cup water

Instructions

1. In medium bowl whisk together all ingredients

except water. Pour into 4-inch ramekin. Generally, if the ramekin is oven-safe, it is also safe to use in pressure cooking. 2. Pour water into Instant Pot. Place steam rack into pot. Carefully place ramekin onto steam rack. Click lid closed. Press the Manual button and set time for 15 minutes. When timer beeps, quick-release the pressure. Serve warm.

Per Serving:

calories: 201 | fat: 14g | protein: 13g | carbs: 3g | net carbs: 2g | fiber: 1g

Egg-Stuffed Avocados

Preparation time: 5 minutes | Cook time: 35 minutes | Serves 2

- ✓ 1 large avocado, halved and pitted
- ✓ 2 small eggs
- ✓ Pink Himalayan sea salt
- ✓ Freshly ground black pepper
- ✓ 1 bacon slice, cooked until crispy and crumbled

Instructions

1. Preheat the oven to 375°F (190°C). 2. Using a small spoon, enlarge the hole of the avocado left by the pit so it is roughly 2 inches in diameter. 3. Place the avocado halves cut-side up on a baking sheet. 4. Crack an egg into the well of each half. Season with salt and pepper. 5. Bake for 30 to 35 minutes, until the yolk reaches your preferred texture, 30 minutes for soft and 35 minutes for hard. 6. Sprinkle the bacon crumbles on top and enjoy!

Per Serving:

calories: 264 | fat: 21g | protein: 10g | carbs: 12g | net carbs: 3g | fiber: 9g

Flappa Jacks

Preparation time: 10 minutes | Cook time: 14 minutes | Serves 6

- ✓ 1 cup blanched almond flour
- ✓ ¼ cup coconut flour
- ✓ 5 large eggs, whisked
- ✓ 3 (1-gram) packets 0g net carb sweetener
- ✓ 1 teaspoon baking powder
- ✓ ⅓ cup unsweetened almond milk
- ✓ ¼ cup vegetable oil

- ✓ 1½ teaspoons pure vanilla extract
- ✓ ⅛ teaspoon salt

Instructions

1. In a large mixing bowl, mix all ingredients together until smooth. 2. In a large nonstick skillet over medium heat, pour desired-sized pancakes and cook 3 to 5 minutes until bubbles form. 3. Flip pancakes and cook another 2 minutes until brown. Repeat as needed to use all batter. Serve.

Per Serving:

calories: 273 | fat: 23g | protein: 10g | carbs: 7g | net carbs: 3g | fiber: 4g

Chicken and Egg Sandwich

Preparation time: 5 minutes | Cook time: 15 minutes | Serves 1

- ✓ 1 (6-ounce / 170-g) boneless, skinless chicken breast
- ✓ ¼ teaspoon salt
- ✓ ⅛ teaspoon pepper
- ✓ ¼ teaspoon garlic powder
- ✓ 2 tablespoons coconut oil, divided
- ✓ 1 egg
- ✓ 1 cup water
- ✓ ¼ avocado
- ✓ 2 tablespoons mayonnaise
- ✓ ¼ cup shredded white Cheddar
- ✓ Salt and pepper, to taste

Instructions

1. Cut chicken breast in half lengthwise. Use meat tenderizer to pound chicken breast until thin. Sprinkle with salt, pepper, and garlic powder, and set aside. 2. Add 1 tablespoon coconut oil to Instant Pot. Press Sauté button, then press Adjust button and set temperature to Less. Once oil is hot, fry the egg, remove, and set aside. Press Cancel button. Press Sauté button, then press Adjust button to set temperature to Normal. Add second tablespoon of coconut oil to Instant Pot and sear chicken on each side for 3 to 4 minutes until golden. 3. Press the Manual button and set time for 8 minutes. While chicken cooks, use fork to mash avocado and then mix in mayo. When timer beeps, quick-release the

pressure. Put chicken on plate and pat dry with paper towel. Use chicken pieces to form a sandwich with egg, cheese, and avocado mayo. Season lightly with salt and pepper.

Per Serving:

calories: 760 | fat: 53g | protein: 52g | carbs: 5g | net carbs: 3g | fiber: 2g

Glazed Chocolate Donuts

Preparation time: 10 minutes | Cook time: 20 minutes | Serves 3

- ✓ Donuts:
- ✓ Coconut oil cooking spray
- ✓ ½ cup almond flour
- ✓ ¼ cup granulated erythritol
- ✓ 2 tablespoons unsweetened cocoa powder
- ✓ ¾ teaspoon baking powder
- ✓ ¼ teaspoon xanthan gum
- ✓ ⅛ teaspoon pink Himalayan sea salt
- ✓ 1 large egg
- ✓ 3 tablespoons heavy (whipping) cream
- ✓ 2 tablespoons butter, melted
- ✓ ¼ teaspoon vanilla extract
- ✓ Glaze:
- ✓ 2 tablespoons powdered erythritol
- ✓ 2 tablespoons butter, melted
- ✓ 2 teaspoons heavy (whipping) cream, warmed

Instructions

1. Preheat the oven to 325°F (163°C). Spray 3 molds of a donut pan with cooking spray. 2. To make the donuts: In a large bowl, combine the almond flour, erythritol, cocoa powder, baking powder, xanthan gum, and salt. Using a whisk, mix well; there should be no clumps. 3. In a small bowl, whisk the egg, cream, melted butter, and vanilla. 4. Pour the wet ingredients into the dry. Whisk until well combined. 5. Portion the dough evenly into these 3 molds. 6. Smooth the donut tops with a wet spoon. 7. Bake for 18 to 20 minutes, until a toothpick inserted in the center comes out clean. 8. Carefully flip the donut pan onto a cooling rack to release the donuts. 9. Let the donuts cool completely before glazing. 10. To make the glaze: In a small bowl, combine the

erythritol, butter, and cream and whisk until smooth.
1Instructions

1. Using a spoon or brush, coat each donut with the glaze mixture, then return it to the cooling rack. If you have enough glaze, double-coat them. 12. Let cool for 30 to 60 minutes. The glaze should be firm to the touch, but you can eat the donuts before the glaze dries, if you can't wait.

Per Serving:

calories: 331 | fat: 33g | protein: 7g | carbs: 7g | net carbs: 4g | fiber: 3g

Overnight "Noats"

Preparation time: 5 minutes | Cook time: 0 minutes | Serves 1

- ✓ 2 tablespoons hulled hemp seeds
- ✓ 1 tablespoon chia seeds
- ✓ ½ scoop collagen powder
- ✓ ½ cup unsweetened nut or seed milk (hemp, almond, coconut, cashew)

Instructions

1. In a small mason jar or glass container, combine the hemp seeds, chia seeds, collagen, and milk. 2. Secure tightly with a lid, shake well, and refrigerate overnight.

Per Serving:

calories: 263 | fat: 19g | protein: 16g | carbs: 7g | net carbs: 2g | fiber: 5g

Meat Waffles/Bagels

Preparation time: 5 minutes | Cook time: 5 to 20 minutes | Serves 4

- ✓ Avocado oil, coconut oil, or butter, for greasing
- ✓ 1 pound (454 g) ground beef, turkey, pork, or bison
- ✓ ½ tablespoon garlic powder
- ✓ ½ tablespoon dried oregano
- ✓ ½ tablespoon paprika
- ✓ Salt and freshly ground black pepper, to taste
- ✓ 4 eggs, sunny-side-up or over-easy, for serving (optional)
- ✓ Sliced cheese, for serving (optional)
- ✓ (You can use any other herbs/spices you like)

Instructions

1. First, determine if you're making meat waffles or meat bagels. Once you figure that out, grab your waffle maker or your bagel baking dish. (If you have neither, perhaps you have a muffin tin? If you have one of those, then you can cook your meat the same way you would the bagels.) Grease the waffle maker or baking dish with oil or butter; if making bagels, preheat the oven to 380°F (193°C). 2. In a bowl, mix the meat with the garlic, oregano, paprika, salt, and pepper. Separate the meat mixture into 4 equal portions and press into the waffle maker or baking dish. 3. The meat will cook 3 to 5 minutes in your waffle maker or 15 to 20 minutes in the oven. (If you're cooking poultry, obviously you need to cook it until completely done.) 4. Once done cooking, let cool slightly, but they should still be slightly warm when you serve them. 5. When ready to serve, place a slice of cheese and an egg on top of each waffle, if desired, and poke the yolk for some extreme yolk porn. Slice the meat bagels in half and place a slice of cheese and an egg inside, if desired. Take a bite like you would a regular bagel, but, warning, yolk may dribble down your face!

Per Serving:

calories: 294 | fat: 19g | protein: 29g | carbs: 2g | net carbs: 2g | fiber: 0g

Bacon Egg Cups

Preparation time: 5 minutes | Cook time: 7 minutes | Serves 4

- ✓ 6 large eggs
- ✓ 2 strips cooked bacon, sliced in ¼-inch wide pieces
- ✓ ½ cup Cheddar cheese, divided
- ✓ ¼ teaspoon sea salt
- ✓ ¼ teaspoon black pepper
- ✓ 1 cup water
- ✓ 1 tablespoon chopped fresh flat leaf parsley

Instructions

1. In a small bowl, beat the eggs. Stir in the cooked bacon, ¼ cup of the cheese, sea salt and pepper. Divide the egg mixture equally among four ramekins

and loosely cover with aluminum foil. 2. Pour the water and place the trivet in the Instant Pot. Place two ramekins on the trivet and stack the other two on the top. 3. Lock the lid. Select the Manual mode and set the cooking time for 7 minutes at High Pressure. When the timer goes off, use a natural pressure release for 10 minutes, then release any remaining pressure. Carefully open the lid. 4. Top each ramekin with the remaining ¼ cup of the cheese. Lock the lid and melt the cheese for 2 minutes. Garnish with the chopped parsley and serve immediately.

Per Serving:

calories: 168 | fat: 12g | protein: 13g | carbs: 1g | net carbs: 1g | fiber: 0g

Spinach and Cheese Frittata

Preparation time: 5 minutes | Cook time: 20 minutes | Serves 4 to 5

✓ 6 eggs
✓ 1 cup chopped spinach
✓ 1 cup shredded full-fat Cheddar cheese
✓ 1 cup shredded full-fat Monterey Jack cheese (optional)
✓ 2 tablespoons coconut oil
✓ 1 cup chopped bell peppers
✓ ½ teaspoon dried parsley
✓ ½ teaspoon dried basil
✓ ½ teaspoon ground turmeric
✓ ½ teaspoon freshly ground black pepper
✓ ½ teaspoon kosher salt

Instructions

1. Pour 1 cup of filtered water into the inner pot of the Instant Pot, then insert the trivet. 2. In a large bowl, combine the eggs, spinach, Cheddar cheese, Monterey Jack cheese, coconut oil, bell peppers, parsley, basil, turmeric, black pepper, and salt, and stir thoroughly. Transfer this mixture into a well-greased Instant Pot-friendly dish. 3. Using a sling if desired, place the dish onto the trivet, and cover loosely with aluminum foil. Close the lid, set the pressure release to Sealing, and select Manual. Set the Instant Pot to 20 minutes on High Pressure,

and let cook. 4. Once cooked, let the pressure naturally disperse from the Instant Pot for about 10 minutes, then carefully switch the pressure release to Venting. 5. Open the Instant Pot, serve, and enjoy!

Per Serving:

calories: 310 | fat: 25g | protein: 18g | carbs: 3g | net carbs: 2g | fiber: 1g

Savory Zucchini Cheddar Waffles

Preparation time: 10 minutes | Cook time: 18 minutes | Makes 4 medium-sized waffles

✓ Waffles:
✓ 2 large zucchini
✓ 2 large eggs
✓ ⅔ cup shredded cheddar cheese (about 2⅔ ounces)
✓ 2 tablespoons coconut flour
✓ ⅛ teaspoon garlic powder
✓ ½ teaspoon red pepper flakes
✓ ¼ teaspoon pink Himalayan salt
✓ For garnish (optinal):
✓ Sour cream
✓ Shredded cheddar cheese
✓ Minced fresh chives

Instructions

1. Preheat a waffle iron on the medium setting. 2. Using a vegetable or cheese grater, grate the zucchini into a large colander set inside of a bowl. Squeeze the excess water out of the grated zucchini using your hands and drain. 3. Add the eggs and cheese to the drained zucchini and combine with a fork. Add the coconut flour, garlic powder, red pepper flakes, and salt and use the fork to combine once more. 4. Open the waffle iron and grease the top and bottom with coconut oil spray. 5. Using a ⅓-cup measuring cup, scoop out some of the batter, place it in the center of the waffle iron, and close the lid. Cook the waffle for 4 to 4½ minutes, until golden brown and fully cooked through. Use a fork to lift it off the iron and set on a plate. 6. Repeat with the remaining batter, making a total of 4 waffles. Garnish with sour cream, shredded cheddar cheese, and/or minced chives, if desired.

calories: 292 | fat: 19g | protein: 20g | carbs: 14g | net carbs: 9g | fiber: 5g

Bacon and Spinach Eggs

Preparation time: 5 minutes | Cook time: 9 minutes | Serves 4

- ✓ 2 tablespoons unsalted butter, divided
- ✓ ½ cup diced bacon
- ✓ ⅓ cup finely diced shallots
- ✓ ⅓ cup chopped spinach, leaves only
- ✓ Pinch of sea salt
- ✓ Pinch of black pepper
- ✓ ½ cup water
- ✓ ¼ cup heavy whipping cream
- ✓ 8 large eggs
- ✓ 1 tablespoon chopped fresh chives, for garnish

Instructions

1. Set the Instant Pot on the Sauté mode and melt 1 tablespoon of the butter. Add the bacon to the pot and sauté for about 4 minutes, or until crispy. Using a slotted spoon, transfer the bacon bits to a bowl and set aside. 2. Add the remaining 1 tablespoon of the butter and shallots to the pot and sauté for about 2 minutes, or until tender. Add the spinach leaves and sauté for 1 minute, or until wilted. Season with sea salt and black pepper and stir. Transfer the spinach to a separate bowl and set aside. 3. Drain the oil from the pot into a bowl. Pour in the water and put the trivet inside. 4. With a paper towel, coat four ramekins with the bacon grease. In each ramekin, place 1 tablespoon of the heavy whipping cream, reserved bacon bits and sautéed spinach. Crack two eggs without breaking the yolks in each ramekin. Cover the ramekins with aluminum foil. Place two ramekins on the trivet and stack the other two on top. 5. Lock the lid. Select the Manual mode and set the cooking time for 2 minutes at Low Pressure. When the timer goes off, use a natural pressure release for 5 minutes, then release any remaining pressure. Carefully open the lid. 6. Carefully take out the ramekins and serve garnished with the chives.

Per Serving:

calories: 320 | fat: 26g | protein: 17g | carbs: 4g | net carbs: 4g | fiber: 0g

Blueberry Mug Muffin

Preparation time: 5 minutes | Cook time: 1 minutes | Serves 1

- ✓ 3 tablespoons blanched almond flour
- ✓ 1 tablespoon coconut flour
- ✓ 1 tablespoon Swerve confectioners'-style sweetener
- ✓ ¼ teaspoon baking powder
- ✓ Pinch of salt
- ✓ 1 large egg
- ✓ 1 tablespoon unsalted butter, softened
- ✓ 1 teaspoon avocado oil
- ✓ ¼ teaspoon vanilla extract
- ✓ 8 blueberries
- ✓ Salted butter, for serving (optional)

Instructions

1. Place the almond flour, coconut flour, sweetener, baking powder, and salt in a medium-large microwave-safe mug and blend with a fork. 2. Add the egg, butter, avocado oil, and vanilla; mix well. 3. Gently stir in the blueberries. Use the back of a spoon to press the batter down and smooth the top. 4. Place the batter-filled mug in the microwave and heat for 1 minute 15 seconds. (The cooking time may vary depending on your microwave. If the muffin is not fully formed after 1 minute 15 seconds, continue cooking in 15-second increments.) Carefully remove the mug from the microwave, it will be hot, flip it upside down over a plate, and allow the muffin to slide out of the mug onto the plate. Place the muffin on its side and slice in half. 5. Spread with butter, if desired, and enjoy!

Per Serving:

1 muffin: calories: 372 | fat: 23g | protein: 12g | carbs: 20g | net carbs: 6g | fiber: 14g

Blackberry Vanilla Cake

Preparation time: 10 minutes | Cook time: 25 minutes | Serves 8

- ✓ 1 cup almond flour

- ✓ 2 eggs
- ✓ ½ cup erythritol
- ✓ 2 teaspoons vanilla extract
- ✓ 1 cup blackberries
- ✓ 4 tablespoons melted butter
- ✓ ¼ cup heavy cream
- ✓ ½ teaspoon baking powder
- ✓ 1 cup water

Instructions

1. In large bowl, mix all ingredients except water. Pour into 7-inch round cake pan or divide into two 4-inch pans, if needed. Cover with foil. 2. Pour water into Instant Pot and place steam rack in bottom. Place pan on steam rack and click lid closed. Press the Cake button and press the Adjust button to set heat to Less. Set time for 25 minutes. 3. When timer beeps, allow a 15-minute natural release then quick-release the remaining pressure. Let cool completely.

Per Serving:

calories: 174 | fat: 15g | protein: 10g | carbs: 17g | net carbs: 15g | fiber: 2g

Bacon-Artichoke Omelet

Preparation time: 10 minutes | Cook time: 10 minutes | Serves 4

- ✓ 6 eggs, beaten
- ✓ 2 tablespoons heavy (whipping) cream
- ✓ 8 bacon slices, cooked and chopped
- ✓ 1 tablespoon olive oil
- ✓ ¼ cup chopped onion
- ✓ ½ cup chopped artichoke hearts (canned, packed in water)
- ✓ Sea salt
- ✓ Freshly ground black pepper

Instructions

1. In a small bowl, whisk together the eggs, heavy cream, and bacon until well blended, and set aside. 2. Place a large skillet over medium-high heat and add the olive oil. 3. Sauté the onion until tender, about 3 minutes. 4. Pour the egg mixture into the skillet, swirling it for 1 minute. 5. Cook the omelet, lifting the edges with a spatula to let the uncooked egg flow underneath, for 2 minutes. 6. Sprinkle the artichoke hearts on top and flip the omelet. Cook for 4 minutes more, until the egg is firm. Flip the omelet over again so the artichoke hearts are on top. 7. Remove from the heat, cut the omelet into quarters, and season with salt and black pepper. Transfer the omelet to plates and serve.

Per Serving:

calories: 435 | fat: 39g | protein: 17g | carbs: 5g | net carbs: 3g | fiber: 2g

Keto Quiche

Preparation time: 10 minutes | Cook time: 1 hour | Makes 1 (6-inch) quiche

- ✓ Crust:
- ✓ 1¼ cups blanched almond flour
- ✓ 1¼ cups grated Parmesan or Gouda cheese
- ✓ ¼ teaspoon fine sea salt
- ✓ 1 large egg, beaten
- ✓ Filling:
- ✓ ½ cup chicken or beef broth (or vegetable broth for vegetarian)
- ✓ 1 cup shredded Swiss cheese (about 4 ounces / 113 g)
- ✓ 4 ounces (113 g) cream cheese (½ cup)
- ✓ 1 tablespoon unsalted butter, melted
- ✓ 4 large eggs, beaten
- ✓ ⅓ cup minced leeks or sliced green onions
- ✓ ¾ teaspoon fine sea salt
- ✓ ⅛ teaspoon cayenne pepper
- ✓ Chopped green onions, for garnish

Instructions

1. Preheat the air fryer to 325°F (163°C). Grease a pie pan. Spray two large pieces of parchment paper with avocado oil and set them on the countertop. 2. Make the crust: In a medium-sized bowl, combine the flour, cheese, and salt and mix well. Add the egg and mix until the dough is well combined and stiff. 3. Place the dough in the center of one of the greased pieces of parchment. Top with the other piece of parchment. Using a rolling pin, roll out the dough into a circle about 1/16 inch thick. 4. Press the pie crust into the prepared pie pan. Place it in the air

fryer and bake for 12 minutes, or until it starts to lightly brown. 5. While the crust bakes, make the filling: In a large bowl, combine the broth, Swiss cheese, cream cheese, and butter. Stir in the eggs, leeks, salt, and cayenne pepper. When the crust is ready, pour the mixture into the crust. 6. Place the quiche in the air fryer and bake for 15 minutes. Turn the heat down to 300ºF (149ºC) and bake for an additional 30 minutes, or until a knife inserted 1 inch from the edge comes out clean. You may have to cover the edges of the crust with foil to prevent burning. 7. Allow the quiche to cool for 10 minutes before garnishing it with chopped green onions and cutting it into wedges. 8. Store leftovers in an airtight container in the refrigerator for up to 4 days or in the freezer for up to a month. Reheat in a preheated 350ºF (177ºC) air fryer for a few minutes, until warmed through.

Per Serving:

calories: 580 | fat: 43g | protein: 31g | carbs: 20g | net carbs: 15g | fiber: 5g

Lettuce Wrapped Chicken Sandwich

Preparation time: 10 minutes | Cook time: 15 minutes | Serves 4

✓   1 tablespoon butter

✓   3 ounces (85 g) scallions, chopped

✓   2 cups ground chicken

✓   ½ teaspoon ground nutmeg

✓   1 tablespoon coconut flour

✓   1 teaspoon salt

✓   1 cup lettuce

Instructions

1. Press the Sauté button on the Instant Pot and melt the butter. Add the chopped scallions, ground chicken and ground nutmeg to the pot and sauté for 4 minutes. Add the coconut flour and salt and continue to sauté for 10 minutes. 2. Fill the lettuce with the ground chicken and transfer it on the plate. Serve immediately.

Per Serving:

calories: 176 | fat: 9g | protein: 21g | carbs: 3g | net carbs: 2g | fiber: 2g

Cheesy Bell Pepper Eggs

Preparation time: 10 minutes | Cook time: 15 minutes | Serves 4

✓   4 medium green bell peppers

✓   3 ounces (85 g) cooked ham, chopped

✓   ¼ medium onion, peeled and chopped

✓   8 large eggs

✓   1 cup mild Cheddar cheese

Instructions

1. Cut the tops off each bell pepper. Remove the seeds and the white membranes with a small knife. Place ham and onion into each pepper. 2. Crack 2 eggs into each pepper. Top with ¼ cup cheese per pepper. Place into the air fryer basket. 3. Adjust the temperature to 390ºF (199ºC) and air fry for 15 minutes. 4. When fully cooked, peppers will be tender and eggs will be firm. Serve immediately.

Per Serving:

calories: 314 | fat: 20g | protein: 25g | carbs: 7g | net carbs: 5g | fiber: 2g

Pumpkin Coconut Flour Pancakes

Preparation time: 5 minutes | Cook time: 10 minutes | Serves 6

✓   6 large eggs

✓   ½ cup canned unsweetened pumpkin purée

✓   6 tablespoons (1½ ounces / 43 g) coconut flour

✓   ¼ cup unsweetened coconut milk

✓   ⅓ cup avocado oil

✓   ½ cup erythritol

✓   1½ tablespoons pumpkin pie spice

✓   1 teaspoon baking powder

✓   1 teaspoon vanilla extract

Instructions

1. In a blender, combine all the ingredients and purée until smooth. 2. Let the batter sit for 15 to 20 minutes to thicken and stabilize. (This will help with consistency and make the pancakes easier to flip.) 3. Heat an oiled skillet over medium heat. Working in batches, add 2 tablespoons (⅛ cup) batter for each pancake. Don't make them larger than 3 inches across, otherwise they will be hard to flip. Cover with

a lid and when bubbles form on the edges, 1 to 2 minutes, flip and cook on the second side for 1 to 2 minutes. 4. Repeat with the remaining batter.

Per Serving:

calories: 234 | fat: 18g | protein: 8g | carbs: 12g | net carbs: 4g | fiber: 8g

Almond and Vanilla Pancakes

Preparation time: 10 minutes | Cook time: 15 minutes | serves 4

- ✓ ⅔ cup unsweetened almond milk
- ✓ 1 tablespoon apple cider vinegar
- ✓ 4 tablespoons coconut oil or vegan butter
- ✓ 1 teaspoon vanilla extract
- ✓ 1 cup coconut flour
- ✓ 1 cup almond flour
- ✓ 2 tablespoons ground flaxseed
- ✓ ½ teaspoon baking powder
- ✓ Coconut oil cooking spray
- ✓ Almond slivers, for serving
- ✓ Vegan butter or coconut oil, for serving
- ✓ Sugar free maple syrup for topping

Instructions

1. Preheat the oven to a warming setting. 2. Combine the almond milk, vinegar, coconut oil, and vanilla in a high-powered blender and blend until thoroughly amalgamated. 3. Add the coconut flour, almond flour, flaxseed, and baking powder. Blend for 3 full minutes until the batter is full and fluffy. If the batter seems too thick, slowly add a few tablespoons of water to thin it out. Set the mixture aside. 4. Heat a medium skillet over medium-low heat and coat it with coconut oil spray to prevent sticking. 5. Once the skillet is hot, pour a small portion of batter into the pan, and cook for about 3 minutes (or until the top of the batter stops bubbling). 6. Flip the pancake and cook until toasted on the opposite side. 7. Place the finished pancake on a warming rack in the oven to keep warm. 8. Repeat steps 5 to 7 until all of the batter has been cooked. 9. Top the pancakes with almond slivers and vegan butter. Drizzle with the maple syrup and serve.

Per Serving:

calories: 426 | fat: 33g | protein: 11g | carbs: 28g | net carbs: 12g | fiber: 16g

Bacon Cheddar Bites

Preparation time: 15 minutes | Cook time: 3 minutes | Serves 2

- ✓ 2 tablespoons coconut flour
- ✓ ½ cup shredded Cheddar cheese
- ✓ 2 teaspoons coconut cream
- ✓ 2 bacon slices, cooked
- ✓ ½ teaspoon dried parsley
- ✓ 1 cup water, for cooking

Instructions

1. In the mixing bowl, mix up coconut flour, Cheddar cheese, coconut cream, and dried parsley. 2. Then chop the cooked bacon and add it in the mixture. 3. Stir it well. 4. Pour water and insert the trivet in the instant pot. 5. Line the trivet with baking paper. 6. After this, make the small balls (bites) from the cheese mixture and put them on the prepared trivet. 7. Cook the meal for 3 minutes on Manual mode (High Pressure). 8. Then make a quick pressure release and cool the cooked meal well.

Per Serving:

calories: 260 | fat: 19g | protein: 15g | carbs: 6g | net carbs: 3g | fiber: 3g

Protein Waffles

Preparation time: 5 minutes | Cook time: 13 minutes | Makes 3 medium-sized waffles

- ✓ Waffles:
- ✓ 4 large eggs
- ✓ ¼ cup natural peanut butter
- ✓ ¼ cup mascarpone cheese
- ✓ ¼ cup unsweetened almond milk 1 scoop unflavored whey protein powder
- ✓ 2 tablespoons unsalted butter, melted
- ✓ Toppings (Optional):
- ✓ Sugar-free maple syrup
- ✓ Natural peanut butter
- ✓ Whipped cream

Instructions

1. Preheat a waffle iron on the medium setting. 2. Put

all the waffle ingredients in a large mixing bowl and combine using a whisk or an electric hand mixer. 3. Open the waffle iron and grease the top and bottom with coconut oil spray. 4. Using a ½-cup measuring cup, scoop up some of the batter and pour it into the center of the waffle iron. Close the lid and allow the waffle to cook for 4 to 4½ minutes, until golden brown. 5. Repeat with the remaining batter, making a total of 3 waffles. 6. Serve the waffles with maple syrup, peanut butter, and/or whipped cream, if desired.

Per Serving:

calories: 409 | fat: 33g | protein: 24g | carbs: 5g | net carbs: 3g | fiber: 2g

Eggs Benedict

Preparation time: 5 minutes | Cook time: 1 minute | Serves 3

- ✓ 1 teaspoon butter
- ✓ 3 eggs
- ✓ ¼ teaspoon salt
- ✓ ½ teaspoon ground black pepper
- ✓ 1 cup water
- ✓ 3 turkey bacon slices, fried

Instructions

1. Grease the eggs molds with the butter and crack the eggs inside. Sprinkle with salt and ground black pepper. 2. Pour the water and insert the trivet in the Instant Pot. Put the eggs molds on the trivet. 3. Set the lid in place. Select the Manual mode and set the cooking time for 1 minute on High Pressure. When the timer goes off, do a quick pressure release. Carefully open the lid. 4. Transfer the eggs onto the plate. Top the eggs with the fried bacon slices.

Per Serving:

calories: 94 | fat: 6g | protein: 9g | carbs: 1g | net carbs: 0g | fiber: 0g

Quickly Blue Cheese Omelet

Preparation time: 10 minutes | Cook time: 10 minutes | Serves 2

- ✓ 4 eggs
- ✓ Salt, to taste

- ✓ 1 tablespoon sesame oil
- ✓ ½ cup blue cheese, crumbled
- ✓ 1 tomato, thinly sliced

Instructions

1. In a mixing bowl, beat the eggs and season with salt. 2. Set a sauté pan over medium heat and warm the oil. Add in the eggs and cook as you swirl the eggs around the pan using a spatula. Cook eggs until partially set. Top with cheese; fold the omelet in half to enclose filling. Decorate with tomato and serve while warm.

Per Serving:

calories: 321 | fat: 26g | protein: 16g | carbs: 4g | net carbs: 4g | fiber: 1g

Easy Skillet Pancakes

Preparation time: 5 minutes | Cook time: 5 minutes | Makes 8 pancakes

- ✓ 8 ounces (227 g) cream cheese
- ✓ 8 eggs
- ✓ 2 tablespoons coconut flour
- ✓ 2 teaspoons baking powder
- ✓ 1 teaspoon ground cinnamon
- ✓ ½ teaspoon vanilla extract
- ✓ 1 teaspoon liquid stevia or sweetener of choice (optional)
- ✓ 2 tablespoons butter

Instructions

1. In a blender, combine the cream cheese, eggs, coconut flour, baking powder, cinnamon, vanilla, and stevia (if using). Blend until smooth. 2. In a large skillet over medium heat, melt the butter. 3. Use half the mixture to pour four evenly sized pancakes and cook for about a minute, until you see bubbles on top. Flip the pancakes and cook for another minute. Remove from the pan and add more butter or oil to the skillet if needed. Repeat with the remaining batter. 4. Top with butter and eat right away, or freeze the pancakes in a freezer-safe resealable bag with sheets of parchment in between, for up to 1 month.

Per Serving:

1 pancake: calories: 179 | fat: 15g | protein: 8g | carbs:

3g | net carbs: 2g | fiber: 1g

Parmesan Baked Eggs

Preparation time: 5 minutes | Cook time: 10 minutes | Serves 1

- ✓ 1 tablespoon butter, cut into small pieces
- ✓ 2 tablespoons keto-friendly low-carb Marinara sauce
- ✓ 3 eggs
- ✓ 2 tablespoons grated Parmesan cheese
- ✓ ¼ teaspoon Italian seasoning
- ✓ 1 cup water

Instructions

1. Place the butter pieces on the bottom of the oven-safe bowl. Spread the marinara sauce over the butter. Crack the eggs on top of the marinara sauce and top with the cheese and Italian seasoning. 2. Cover the bowl with aluminum foil. Pour the water and insert the trivet in the Instant Pot. Put the bowl on the trivet. 3. Set the lid in place. Select the Manual mode and set the cooking time for 10 minutes on Low Pressure. When the timer goes off, do a quick pressure release. Carefully open the lid. 4. Let the eggs cool for 5 minutes before serving.

Per Serving:

calories: 375 | fat: 30g | protein: 23g | carbs: 2g | net carbs: 2g | fiber: 0g

Avocado and Eggs

Preparation time: 10 minutes | Cook time: 20 minutes | Serves 4

- ✓ 2 avocados, peeled, halved lengthwise, and pitted
- ✓ 4 large eggs
- ✓ 1 (4-ounce) chicken breast, cooked and shredded
- ✓ ¼ cup Cheddar cheese
- ✓ Sea salt
- ✓ Freshly ground black pepper

Instructions

1. Preheat the oven to 425°F. 2. Take a spoon and hollow out each side of the avocado halves until the hole is about twice the original size. 3. Place the avocado halves in an 8-by-8-inch baking dish, hollow-side up. 4. Crack an egg into each hollow and divide the shredded chicken between each avocado half. Sprinkle the cheese on top of each and season lightly with the salt and pepper. 5. Bake the avocados until the eggs are cooked through, about 15 to 20 minutes. 6. Serve immediately.

Per Serving:

calories: 324 | fat: 25g | protein: 19g | carbs: 8g | net carbs: 3g | fiber: 5g

Cinnamon Rolls

Preparation time: 10 minutes | Cook time: 20 minutes | Makes 12 rolls

- ✓ 2½ cups shredded Mozzarella cheese
- ✓ 2 ounces (57 g) cream cheese, softened
- ✓ 1 cup blanched finely ground almond flour
- ✓ ½ teaspoon vanilla extract
- ✓ ½ cup confectioners' erythritol
- ✓ 1 tablespoon ground cinnamon

Instructions

1. In a large microwave-safe bowl, combine Mozzarella cheese, cream cheese, and flour. Microwave the mixture on high 90 seconds until cheese is melted. 2. Add vanilla extract and erythritol, and mix 2 minutes until a dough forms. 3. Once the dough is cool enough to work with your hands, about 2 minutes, spread it out into a 12 × 4-inch rectangle on ungreased parchment paper. Evenly sprinkle dough with cinnamon. 4. Starting at the long side of the dough, roll lengthwise to form a log. Slice the log into twelve even pieces. 5. Divide rolls between two ungreased round nonstick baking dishes. Place one dish into air fryer basket. Adjust the temperature to 375°F (191°C) and bake for 10 minutes. 6. Cinnamon rolls will be done when golden around the edges and mostly firm. Repeat with second dish. Allow rolls to cool in dishes 10 minutes before serving.

Per Serving:

calories: 123 | fat: 9g | protein: 7g | carbs: 3g | net carbs: 2g | fiber: 1g

CHAPTER 2 Poultry and Meat

Four Horsemen Butter Chicken

Preparation time: 10 minutes | Cook time: 27 minutes | Serves 8

- ✓ 1 tablespoon unsalted butter
- ✓ 1 tablespoon olive oil
- ✓ 1 medium onion, peeled and diced
- ✓ 3 cloves garlic, peeled and minced
- ✓ 2 teaspoons peeled and grated fresh ginger
- ✓ 2 pounds boneless, skinless chicken breasts, cooked and cut into ¾" chunks
- ✓ 3 ounces tomato paste
- ✓ 3 ounces red curry paste
- ✓ 1 tablespoon garam masala
- ✓ 1 teaspoon chili powder
- ✓ 1 teaspoon mustard seeds
- ✓ 1 teaspoon ground coriander
- ✓ 1 teaspoon curry
- ✓ 1 teaspoon salt
- ✓ ⅛ teaspoon black pepper
- ✓ 1 (14-ounce) can unsweetened coconut milk
- ✓ 1 teaspoon chopped cilantro

Instructions

1. In a large skillet over medium-high heat, heat butter and olive oil. Add onion and fry until soft, about 3–5 minutes. Mix in garlic and ginger. Cook 1–2 minutes more. 2. Add cooked chicken to skillet. Add tomato paste, red curry paste, garam masala, chili powder, mustard seeds, coriander, and curry. Add salt and pepper. Stir until well mixed and chicken cubes are well coated. 3. Stir in coconut milk and bring to boil. Reduce heat. Cover and simmer 20 minutes. 4. Remove from heat. Let cool 10 minutes and serve warm with cilantro sprinkled on top.

Per Serving:

calories: 303 | fat: 15g | protein: 28g | carbs: 12g | net carbs: 9g | fiber: 3g

Cream of Mushroom-Stuffed Chicken

Preparation time: 10 minutes | Cook time: 45 minutes | Serves 4

- ✓ 3 tablespoons coconut oil, avocado oil, or ghee
- ✓ 7 ounces (200 g) cremini mushrooms, chopped
- ✓ 4 cloves garlic, minced
- ✓ 3 teaspoons dried parsley, divided
- ✓ ¾ teaspoon finely ground sea salt, divided
- ✓ ¼ teaspoon ground black pepper
- ✓ 1 pound (455 g) boneless, skin-on chicken breasts
- ✓ 1 teaspoon onion powder
- ✓ 1 teaspoon garlic powder
- ✓ ½ cup (120 ml) milk (nondairy or regular)
- ✓ 4 cups (280 g) spinach, for serving

Instructions

1. Preheat the oven to 400°F (205°C). Line a rimmed baking sheet with parchment paper or a silicone baking mat. 2. Heat the oil in a large frying pan over medium heat. Add the mushrooms, garlic, 2 teaspoons of the parsley, ¼ teaspoon of the salt, and the pepper. Toss to coat and sauté for 10 minutes. 3. Meanwhile, slice each chicken breast horizontally, stopping the knife about ½ inch (Instructions 1.25 cm) from the opposite side, so that it opens like a book; be careful not to slice the breasts all the way through. The best way to do this is to use a sharp knife and place your palm on the top of the breast to hold it steady. 4. Place the chicken breasts on the lined baking sheet and open them up. Place one-quarter of the mushroom mixture in the middle of each opened breast. If there is leftover mushroom mixture, simply drop it into the pan, around the chicken. 5. Fold over the chicken breasts to cover the filling. Dust the stuffed breasts with the garlic powder, onion powder, remaining 1 teaspoon of parsley, and remaining ½ teaspoon of salt. 6. Pour the milk between the chicken breasts, directly into the pan. 7. Bake for 30 to 35 minutes, until the internal temperature of the chicken reaches 165°F (74°C). 8. Divide the spinach among 4 dinner plates.

Divide the stuffed chicken breasts among the plates, drizzle the spinach with the creamy pan juices, and enjoy! (Note: If you did not end up with one breast half per person in the package, cut the stuffed breasts into portions and divide them equally among the plates.)

Per Serving:

calories: 388 | fat: 24g | protein: 38g | carbs: 7g | net carbs: 4g | fiber: 2g

Butter Chicken

Preparation time: 10 minutes | Cook time: 45 minutes | Serves 4

- ✓ ⅓ cup (70 g) coconut oil
- ✓ 1⅓ pounds (600 g) boneless, skinless chicken thighs, cubed
- ✓ ½ cup (70 g) sliced yellow onions
- ✓ 2 small cloves garlic, minced
- ✓ 1 (1-in/2.5-cm) piece fresh ginger root, grated
- ✓ 1 (14½-ounce/400-g/428-ml) can diced tomatoes
- ✓ 1 cup (240 ml) chicken bone broth
- ✓ 1 bay leaf
- ✓ 1 tablespoon garam masala or curry powder
- ✓ 1 teaspoon ground cumin
- ✓ 1 teaspoon finely ground gray sea salt
- ✓ ½ teaspoon ground coriander
- ✓ ¼ teaspoon ground cloves
- ✓ ⅛ teaspoon ground black pepper
- ✓ ⅛ teaspoon ground cardamom
- ✓ ⅓ cup (80 ml) full-fat coconut milk
- ✓ 3 tablespoons blanched almond flour
- ✓ 1 tablespoon fresh lemon juice
- ✓ Handful of fresh cilantro, roughly chopped, for garnish
- ✓ Sliced green onions, for garnish

Instructions

1. Melt the coconut oil in a large saucepan or deep sauté pan over medium-high heat. Add the cubed chicken to the pan and cook for 10 minutes, or until the chicken is no longer pink. 2. Add the onions, garlic, and ginger and continue to cook for 5 minutes, until fragrant. 3. Add the tomatoes, bone broth, bay

leaf, garam masala, cumin, salt, coriander, cloves, pepper, and cardamom and give everything a stir. Cover and bring to a boil, then reduce the heat to low and lightly simmer for 20 minutes. 4. Stir in the coconut milk, almond flour, and lemon juice. Increase the heat to medium-high and cook for 5 minutes, until slightly thickened. 5. Remove the bay leaf. Divide the chicken and sauce among 4 serving bowls. Top with cilantro and green onions and enjoy.

Per Serving:

calories: 450 | fat: 31g | protein: 34g | carbs: 8g | net carbs: 5g | fiber: 2g

Chicken Breasts with Cheddar & Pepperoni

Preparation time: 10 minutes | Cook time: 35 minutes | Serves 4

- ✓ 12 ounces canned tomato sauce
- ✓ 1 tablespoon olive oil
- ✓ 4 chicken breast halves, skinless and boneless
- ✓ Salt and ground black pepper, to taste
- ✓ 1 teaspoon dried oregano
- ✓ 4 ounces cheddar cheese, sliced
- ✓ 1 teaspoon garlic powder
- ✓ 2 ounces pepperoni, sliced

Instructions

1. Preheat your oven to 390°F. In a bowl, combine chicken with oregano, salt, garlic, and pepper. 2. Heat a pan with the olive oil over medium heat, add in the chicken, cook each side for 2 minutes, and remove to a baking dish. Top with the cheddar cheese slices spread the sauce, then cover with pepperoni slices. Bake for 30 minutes. Serve warm garnished with fresh oregano if desired.

Per Serving:

calories: 348 | fat: 24g | protein: 29g | carbs: 4g | net carbs: 4g | fiber: 0g

Lemon Garlic Chicken

Preparation time: 20 minutes | Cook time: 30 minutes | Serves 6

- ✓ 2 pounds (907 g) skinless chicken thighs
- ✓ 1 tablespoon avocado oil

- ✓ 1 teaspoon minced garlic
- ✓ ½ teaspoon ground coriander
- ✓ 1 teaspoon lemon zest
- ✓ 1 teaspoon lemon juice
- ✓ ⅓ cup chicken broth
- ✓ 1 cup water

Instructions

1. Pour water and insert the steamer rack in the instant pot. Pour water and chicken broth in the instant pot bowl. 2. Put the chicken thighs in the bowl and sprinkle them with avocado oil, minced garlic, ground coriander, lemon zest, and lemon juice. 3. Then shake the chicken thighs gently and transfer them on the steamer rack. 4. Close and seal the lid. 5. Cook the chicken for 15 minutes on Manual mode (High Pressure). Then make a quick pressure release and transfer the chicken thighs on the plate.

Per Serving:

calories: 294 | fat: 12g | protein: 44g | carbs: 0g | net carbs: 0g | fiber: 0g

Zesty Grilled Chicken

Preparation time: 5 minutes | Cook time: 20 minutes | Serves 8

- ✓ 2½ pounds chicken thighs and drumsticks
- ✓ 1 tablespoon coconut aminos
- ✓ 1 tablespoon apple cider vinegar
- ✓ A pinch of red pepper flakes
- ✓ Salt and black pepper, to taste
- ✓ ½ teaspoonground ginger
- ✓ ⅓ cup butter
- ✓ 1 garlic clove, minced
- ✓ 1 teaspoon lime zest
- ✓ ½ cup warm water

Instructions

1. In a blender, combine the butter with water, salt, ginger, vinegar, garlic, pepper, lime zest, aminos, and pepper flakes. Pat the chicken dry, lay on a pan, and top with zesty marinade. Refrigerate for 1 hour. 2. Set the chicken pieces skin side down on a preheated grill over medium heat, cook for 10 minutes, turn, brush with some marinade, and cook for 10 minutes. Split among serving plates and enjoy.

Per Serving:

calories: 286 | fat: 14g | protein: 37g | carbs: 3g | net carbs: 3g | fiber: 0g

Chicken Paillard

Preparation time: 10 minutes | Cook time: 10 minutes | Serves 2

- ✓ 2 large eggs, room temperature
- ✓ 1 tablespoon water
- ✓ ½ cup powdered Parmesan cheese (about 1½ ounces / 43 g) or pork dust
- ✓ 2 teaspoons dried thyme leaves
- ✓ 1 teaspoon ground black pepper
- ✓ 2 (5 ounces / 142 g) boneless, skinless chicken breasts, pounded to ½ inch thick
- ✓ Lemon Butter Sauce:
- ✓ 2 tablespoons unsalted butter, melted
- ✓ 2 teaspoons lemon juice
- ✓ ¼ teaspoon finely chopped fresh thyme leaves, plus more for garnish
- ✓ ⅛ teaspoon fine sea salt
- ✓ Lemon slices, for serving

Instructions

1. Spray the air fryer basket with avocado oil. Preheat the air fryer to 390°F (199°C). 2. Beat the eggs in a shallow dish, then add the water and stir well. 3. In a separate shallow dish, mix together the Parmesan, thyme, and pepper until well combined. 4. One at a time, dip the chicken breasts in the eggs and let any excess drip off, then dredge both sides of the chicken in the Parmesan mixture. As you finish, set the coated chicken in the air fryer basket. 5. Roast the chicken in the air fryer for 5 minutes, then flip the chicken and cook for another 5 minutes, or until cooked through and the internal temperature reaches 165°F (74°C). 6. While the chicken cooks, make the lemon butter sauce: In a small bowl, mix together all the sauce ingredients until well combined. 7. Plate the chicken and pour the sauce over it. Garnish with chopped fresh thyme and serve with lemon slices. 8. Store leftovers in an airtight container in the refrigerator for up to 4 days. Reheat in a preheated 390°F (199°C) air fryer for 5 minutes,

or until heated through.

Per Serving:

calories: 496 | fat: 31g | protein: 48g | carbs: 5g | net carbs: 5g | fiber: 0g

Parmesan Carbonara Chicken

Preparation time: 15 minutes | Cook time: 25 minutes | Serves 5

- ✓ 1 pound (454 g) chicken, skinless, boneless, chopped
- ✓ 1 cup heavy cream
- ✓ 1 cup chopped spinach
- ✓ 2 ounces (57 g) Parmesan, grated
- ✓ 1 teaspoon ground black pepper
- ✓ 1 tablespoon coconut oil
- ✓ 2 ounces (57 g) bacon, chopped

Instructions

1. Put the coconut oil and chopped chicken in the instant pot. 2. Sauté the chicken for 10 minutes. Stir it from time to time. 3. Then add ground black pepper, and spinach. Stir the mixture well and sauté for 5 minutes more. 4. Then add heavy cream and Parmesan. Close and seal the lid. 5. Cook the meal on Manual mode (High Pressure) for 10 minutes. Allow the natural pressure release for 10 minutes.

Per Serving:

calories: 343 | fat: 22g | protein: 35g | carbs: 2g | net carbs: 2g | fiber: 0g

Barbecue Shredded Chicken

Preparation time: 5 minutes | Cook time: 25 minutes | Serves 4

- ✓ 1 (5-pound / 2.2-kg) whole chicken
- ✓ 3 teaspoons salt
- ✓ 1 teaspoon pepper
- ✓ 1 teaspoon dried parsley
- ✓ 1 teaspoon garlic powder
- ✓ ½ medium onion, cut into 3 to 4 large pieces
- ✓ 1 cup water
- ✓ ½ cup sugar-free barbecue sauce, divided

Instructions

1. Scatter the chicken with salt, pepper, parsley, and garlic powder. Put the onion pieces inside the chicken cavity. 2. Pour the water into the Instant Pot and insert the trivet. Place seasoned chicken on the trivet. Brush with half of the barbecue sauce. 3. Lock the lid. Select the Manual mode and set the cooking time for 25 minutes at High Pressure. 4. When the timer beeps, perform a natural pressure release for 10 minutes, then release any remaining pressure. Carefully remove the lid. 5. Using a clean brush, add the remaining half of the sauce to chicken. For crispy skin or thicker sauce, you can broil in the oven for 5 minutes until lightly browned. 6. Slice or shred the chicken and serve warm.

Per Serving:

calories: 1054 | fat: 73g | protein: 71g | carbs: 7g | net carbs: 6g | fiber: 1g

Turkey Breast Salad

Preparation time: 10 minutes | Cook time: 15 minutes | Serves 4

- ✓ 1 tablespoon swerve
- ✓ 1 red onion, chopped
- ✓ ¼ cup vinegar
- ✓ ¼ cup olive oil
- ✓ ¼ cup water
- ✓ 1¾ cups raspberries
- ✓ 1 tablespoon Dijon mustard
- ✓ Salt and ground black pepper, to taste
- ✓ 10 ounces baby spinach
- ✓ 2 medium turkey breasts, boneless
- ✓ 4 ounces goat cheese, crumbled
- ✓ ½ cup pecans halves

Instructions

1. In a blender, combine swerve, vinegar, 1 cup raspberries, black pepper, mustard, water, onion, oil, and salt, and ensure well blended. Strain this into a bowl, and set aside. Cut the turkey breast in half, add black pepper and salt, and place skin side down into a pan. 2. Cook for 8 minutes flipping to the other side and cooking for 5 minutes. Split the spinach among plates, spread with the remaining raspberries, pecan halves, and goat cheese. Slice the turkey breasts, put over the salad and top with raspberries vinaigrette and enjoy.

Per Serving:

calories: 584 | fat: 43g | protein: 39g | carbs: 23g | net carbs: 16g | fiber: 7g

Chicken Florentine

Preparation time: 10 minutes | Cook time: 30 minutes | Serves 4

- ✓ 1 pound (454 g) boneless skinless chicken breasts
- ✓ Salt, to taste
- ✓ Freshly ground black pepper, to taste
- ✓ 3 tablespoons butter, divided
- ✓ ¼ white onion, diced
- ✓ 2 garlic cloves, minced
- ✓ 1 cup chicken broth
- ✓ 1 cup heavy (whipping) cream
- ✓ 10 ounces (283 g) fresh spinach, chopped
- ✓ ½ cup grated Parmesan cheese

Instructions

1. Preheat the oven to 200ºF (93ºC). 2. Season the chicken with salt and pepper. In a large skillet over medium heat, melt 1½ tablespoons of butter. Add the chicken and cook for about 5 minutes per side or until browned. Transfer the chicken to an ovenproof dish and keep it warm in the low oven. 3. Return the skillet to the heat and melt the remaining 1½ tablespoons of butter. 4. Add the onion and garlic. Sauté for 5 to 7 minutes until the onion is softened and translucent. 5. Add the chicken broth. Increase the heat to medium high and simmer for about 3 minutes until reduced slightly 6. Stir in the cream and spinach. Cook for 3 to 4 minutes. Transfer the sauce to the baking dish with the chicken. Top with the Parmesan. Increase the oven temperature to 350ºF (180ºC). Cook for about 5 minutes or until the Parmesan browns slightly. Refrigerate leftovers in an airtight container for up to 5 days.

Per Serving:

calories: 489 | fat: 36g | protein: 36g | carbs: 6g | net carbs: 4g | fiber: 2g

Cheese Stuffed Chicken

Preparation time: 15 minutes | Cook time: 20 minutes | Serves 4

- ✓ 12 ounces (340 g) chicken fillet
- ✓ 4 ounces (113 g) provolone cheese, sliced
- ✓ 1 tablespoon cream cheese
- ✓ ½ teaspoon dried cilantro
- ✓ ½ teaspoon smoked paprika
- ✓ 1 cup water, for cooking

Instructions

1. Beat the chicken fillet well and rub it with dried cilantro and smoked paprika. 2. Then spread it with cream cheese and top with Provolone cheese. 3. Roll the chicken fillet into the roll and wrap in the foil. 4. Pour water and insert the rack in the instant pot. 5. Place the chicken roll on the rack. Close and seal the lid. 6. Cook it on Manual mode (High Pressure) for 20 minutes. 7. Make a quick pressure release and slice the chicken roll into the servings.

Per Serving:

calories: 271 | fat: 15g | protein: 32g | carbs: 1g | net carbs: 1g | fiber: 0g

French Garlic Chicken

Preparation time: 30 minutes | Cook time: 27 minutes | Serves 4

- ✓ 2 tablespoon extra-virgin olive oil
- ✓ 1 tablespoon Dijon mustard
- ✓ 1 tablespoon apple cider vinegar
- ✓ 3 cloves garlic, minced
- ✓ 2 teaspoons herbes de Provence
- ✓ ½ teaspoon kosher salt
- ✓ 1 teaspoon black pepper
- ✓ 1 pound (454 g) boneless, skinless chicken thighs, halved crosswise
- ✓ 2 tablespoons butter
- ✓ 8 cloves garlic, chopped
- ✓ ¼ cup heavy whipping cream

Instructions

1. In a small bowl, combine the olive oil, mustard, vinegar, minced garlic, herbes de Provence, salt, and pepper. Use a wire whisk to emulsify the mixture. 2. Pierce the chicken all over with a fork to allow the marinade to penetrate better. Place the chicken in a resealable plastic bag, pour the marinade over, and

seal. Massage until the chicken is well coated. Marinate at room temperature for 30 minutes or in the refrigerator for up to 24 hours. 3. When you are ready to cook, place the butter and chopped garlic in a baking pan and place it in the air fryer basket. Set the air fryer to 400°F (204°C) for 5 minutes, or until the butter has melted and the garlic is sizzling. 4. Add the chicken and the marinade to the seasoned butter. Set the air fryer to 350°F (177°C) for 15 minutes. Use a meat thermometer to ensure the chicken has reached an internal temperature of 165°F (74°C). Transfer the chicken to a plate and cover lightly with foil to keep warm. 5. Add the cream to the pan, stirring to combine with the garlic, butter, and cooking juices. Place the pan in the air fryer basket. Set the air fryer to 350°F (177°C) for 7 minutes. 6. Pour the thickened sauce over the chicken and serve.

Per Serving:

calories: 291 | fat: 20g | protein: 23g | carbs: 4g | net carbs: 3g | fiber: 1g

Biscuit-Topped Chicken Pot Pie

Preparation time: 25 minutes | Cook time: 30 minutes | Serves 4

- ✓ Biscuits:
- ✓ 1 cup almond flour
- ✓ 1½ teaspoons baking powder
- ✓ ½ teaspoon salt
- ✓ 2 tablespoons cold butter, diced into small chunks
- ✓ 2 tablespoons heavy cream
- ✓ 1 large egg
- ✓ 2 ounces (57 g) shredded Mozzarella or Cheddar cheese
- ✓ Filling:
- ✓ 2 tablespoons extra-virgin olive oil
- ✓ ½ small yellow onion, finely chopped
- ✓ 4 ribs celery, diced small (about 1 cup diced celery)
- ✓ 4 ounces (113 g) chopped mushrooms
- ✓ ¼ cup diced carrot (about 1 small carrot)
- ✓ 1½ teaspoons dried thyme
- ✓ 1 teaspoon salt
- ✓ ¼ teaspoon freshly ground black pepper
- ✓ 4 cloves garlic, minced
- ✓ ¼ cup dry white wine or chicken stock
- ✓ 1 cup heavy cream, divided
- ✓ 4 ounces (113 g) cream cheese, room temperature
- ✓ 1 teaspoon Worcestershire sauce
- ✓ 2 cups (4 or 5 thighs) cooked chicken thigh meat, diced

Instructions

1. Preheat the oven to 375°F (190°C). 2. To make the biscuits. In a large bowl, combine the almond flour, baking powder, and salt in a large bowl and mix well. Add the cubed butter and use a fork or your hands to crumble it into the flour mixture until it resembles coarse pebbles. 3. Whisk in the heavy cream, 1 tablespoon at a time. Whisk in the egg and cheese until the mixture forms a smooth dough. Set aside. 4. To make the filling. Heat the olive oil in a large skillet over medium-high heat. Add the onion, celery, mushrooms, carrot, thyme, salt, and pepper and sauté until vegetables are just tender, 5 to 6 minutes. Add the garlic and sauté for an additional 30 seconds. 5. Add the wine or stock, stirring until most of the liquid has evaporated. Whisk in ¾ cup of heavy cream, and bring to just below a simmer. Reduce heat to low and cook, stirring occasionally, for 4 to 5 minutes. 6. In a microwave-safe bowl, combine the remaining ¼ cup of heavy cream, cream cheese, and Worcestershire sauce and microwave on high for 45 to 60 seconds, or until the cream cheese is melted. Whisk until smooth. Add the cream mixture to the vegetable mixture, stirring until smooth. 7. Add the diced chicken and stir to combine. Pour the chicken-and-vegetable mixture into an 8-inch square glass baking dish or pie pan. 8. Form the biscuit dough into 8 balls (the mixture will be sticky), flatten into 8 flat biscuits, and place atop the chicken and vegetables. Bake until bubbly and biscuits are golden brown, 16 to 18 minutes.

Per Serving:

calories: 776 | fat: 68g | protein: 32g | carbs: 13g |

net carbs: 9g | fiber: 4g

Chicken with Parmesan Topping

Preparation time: 15 minutes | Cook time: 40 minutes | Serves 4

- ✓ 4 chicken breast halves, skinless and boneless
- ✓ Salt and black pepper, to taste
- ✓ ¼ cup green chilies, chopped
- ✓ 5 bacon slices, chopped
- ✓ 6 ounces cream cheese
- ✓ ¼ cup onion, chopped
- ✓ ½ cup mayonnaise
- ✓ ½ cup Grana Padano cheese, grated
- ✓ 1 cup cheddar cheese, grated
- ✓ 2 ounces pork rinds, crushed
- ✓ 2 tablespoons olive oil
- ✓ ½ cup Parmesan cheese, shredded

Instructions

1. Season the chicken with salt and pepper. Heat the olive oil in a pan over medium heat and fry the chicken for approximately 4-6 minutes until cooked through with no pink showing. Remove to a baking dish. 2. In the same pan, fry bacon until crispy and remove to a plate. Sauté the onion for 3 minutes, until soft. Remove from heat, add in the fried bacon, cream cheese, 1 cup of water, Grana Padano cheese, mayonnaise, chilies, and cheddar cheese, and spread over the chicken. 3. Bake in the oven for 10-15 minutes at 370°F. Remove and sprinkle with mixed Parmesan cheese and pork rinds and return to the oven. Bake for another 10-15 minutes until the cheese melts. Serve immediately.

Per Serving:

calories: 773 | fat: 57g | protein: 58g | carbs: 7g | net carbs: 6g | fiber: 1g

Parmesan Wings with Yogurt Sauce

Preparation time: 5 minutes | Cook time: 20 minutes | Serves 6

- ✓ For the Dipping Sauce
- ✓ 1 cup plain yogurt
- ✓ 1 teaspoon fresh lemon juice
- ✓ Salt and black pepper to taste
- ✓ For the Wings
- ✓ 2 pounds (907 g) chicken wings
- ✓ Salt and black pepper to taste
- ✓ Cooking spray
- ✓ ½ cup melted butter
- ✓ ½ cup Hot sauce
- ✓ ¼ cup grated Parmesan cheese

Instructions

1. Mix the yogurt, lemon juice, salt, and black pepper in a bowl. Chill while making the chicken. 2. Preheat oven to 400°F and season wings with salt and black pepper. Line them on a baking sheet and grease lightly with cooking spray. Bake for 20 minutes until golden brown. Mix butter, hot sauce, and Parmesan cheese in a bowl. Toss chicken in the sauce to evenly coat and plate. Serve with yogurt dipping sauce and celery strips.

Per Serving:

calories: 435 | fat: 31g | protein: 33g | carbs: 6g | net carbs: 4g | fiber: 2g

Bacon-Wrapped Stuffed Chicken Breasts

Preparation time: 15 minutes | Cook time: 30 minutes | Serves 4

- ✓ ½ cup chopped frozen spinach, thawed and squeezed dry
- ✓ ¼ cup cream cheese, softened
- ✓ ¼ cup grated Parmesan cheese
- ✓ 1 jalapeño, seeded and chopped
- ✓ ½ teaspoon kosher salt
- ✓ 1 teaspoon black pepper
- ✓ 2 large boneless, skinless chicken breasts, butterflied and pounded to ½-inch thickness
- ✓ 4 teaspoons salt-free Cajun seasoning
- ✓ 6 slices bacon

Instructions

1. In a small bowl, combine the spinach, cream cheese, Parmesan cheese, jalapeño, salt, and pepper. Stir until well combined. 2. Place the butterflied chicken breasts on a flat surface. Spread the cream cheese mixture evenly across each piece of chicken. Starting with the narrow end, roll up each chicken

breast, ensuring the filling stays inside. Season chicken with the Cajun seasoning, patting it in to ensure it sticks to the meat. 3. Wrap each breast in 3 slices of bacon. Place in the air fryer basket. Set the air fryer to 350°F (177°C) for 30 minutes. Use a meat thermometer to ensure the chicken has reached an internal temperature of 165°F (74°C). 4. Let the chicken stand 5 minutes before slicing each rolled-up breast in half to serve.

Per Serving:

calories: 467 | fat: 28g | protein: 49g | carbs: 3g | net carbs: 3g | fiber: 1g

Chicken Kiev

Preparation time: 15 minutes | Cook time: 25 minutes | Serves 4

- ✓ 1 cup (2 sticks) unsalted butter, softened (or butter-flavored coconut oil for dairy-free)
- ✓ 2 tablespoons lemon juice
- ✓ 2 tablespoons plus 1 teaspoon chopped fresh parsley leaves, divided, plus more for garnish
- ✓ 2 tablespoons chopped fresh tarragon leaves
- ✓ 3 cloves garlic, minced
- ✓ 1 teaspoon fine sea salt, divided
- ✓ 4 (4-ounce / 113-g) boneless, skinless chicken breasts
- ✓ 2 large eggs
- ✓ 2 cups pork dust
- ✓ 1 teaspoon ground black pepper
- ✓ Sprig of fresh parsley, for garnish
- ✓ Lemon slices, for serving

Instructions

1. Spray the air fryer basket with avocado oil. Preheat the air fryer to 350°F (177°C). 2. In a medium-sized bowl, combine the butter, lemon juice, 2 tablespoons of the parsley, the tarragon, garlic, and ¼ teaspoon of the salt. Cover and place in the fridge to harden for 7 minutes. 3. While the butter mixture chills, place one of the chicken breasts on a cutting board. With a sharp knife held parallel to the cutting board, make a 1-inch-wide incision at the top of the breast. Carefully cut into the breast to form a large pocket, leaving a ½-inch border along the sides and bottom.

Repeat with the other 3 breasts. 4. Stuff one-quarter of the butter mixture into each chicken breast and secure the openings with toothpicks. 5. Beat the eggs in a small shallow dish. In another shallow dish, combine the pork dust, the remaining 1 teaspoon of parsley, the remaining ¾ teaspoon of salt, and the pepper. 6. One at a time, dip the chicken breasts in the egg, shake off the excess egg, and dredge the breasts in the pork dust mixture. Use your hands to press the pork dust onto each breast to form a nice crust. If you desire a thicker coating, dip it again in the egg and pork dust. As you finish, spray each coated chicken breast with avocado oil and place it in the air fryer basket. 7. Roast the chicken in the air fryer for 15 minutes, flip the breasts, and cook for another 10 minutes, or until the internal temperature of the chicken is 165°F (74°C) and the crust is golden brown. 8. Serve garnished with chopped fresh parsley and a parsley sprig, with lemon slices on the side. 9. Store leftovers in an airtight container in the refrigerator for up to 4 days or in the freezer for up to a month. Reheat in a preheated 350°F (177°C) air fryer for 5 minutes, or until heated through.

Per Serving:

calories: 569 | fat: 40g | protein: 48g | carbs: 3g | net carbs: 3g | fiber: 0g

Mezze Cake

Preparation time: 10 minutes | Cook time: 35 minutes | Serves 2 to 4

- ✓ Nonstick cooking spray
- ✓ 2 coconut wraps (one of them is optional)
- ✓ 1 small eggplant, thinly sliced lengthwise
- ✓ Salt, to taste
- ✓ 1 zucchini, thinly sliced lengthwise
- ✓ 1 (8-ounce / 227-g) jar sun-dried tomatoes packed in olive oil (do not discard oil), chopped or whole
- ✓ ½ (14-ounce / 397-g) can quartered artichoke hearts
- ✓ ½ cup cauliflower rice
- ✓ ¼ cup black olives, pitted and coarsely

chopped

- ✓ 2 precooked sugar-free chicken sausages, cut into bite-size pieces
- ✓ 1 tablespoon dried oregano or marjoram
- ✓ ½ tablespoon garlic powder
- ✓ Freshly ground black pepper, to taste

Instructions

1. Preheat the oven to 350°F (180°C). Coat a shallow baking dish with nonstick spray and place a coconut wrap in the bottom. 2. Sprinkle the eggplant with ½ teaspoon of salt and let sit for 5 minutes to let the moisture come to the surface. Get a damp towel and wipe off the salt and excess water from the eggplant. 3. Lay the eggplant slices on top of the coconut wrap, then lay the zucchini slices on top of the eggplant. Next add the sun-dried tomatoes and drizzle in the olive oil they're packed in. Sprinkle in the artichoke hearts, then add the cauliflower rice. Scatter the olives on top, then shower the chicken sausage over all the vegetables. Season everything with the oregano, garlic powder, salt, and pepper. 4. Place another coconut wrap over the top of everything, if desired, and bake this vegetable layer "cake" in the oven for about 25 minutes, or until the vegetables are a bit wilted. 5. Turn the oven to broil and cook for another 5 minutes, or until the top is crisp. 6. Remove from the oven and let cool before slicing and serving.

Per Serving:

calories: 510 | fat: 38g | protein: 17g | carbs: 25g | net carbs: 13g | fiber: 12g

Coconut Chicken

Preparation time: 10 minutes | Cook time: 25 minutes | Serves 4

- ✓ 2 tablespoons olive oil
- ✓ 4 (4-ounce) chicken breasts, cut into 2-inch chunks
- ✓ ½ cup chopped sweet onion
- ✓ 1 cup coconut milk
- ✓ 1 tablespoon curry powder
- ✓ 1 teaspoon ground cumin
- ✓ 1 teaspoon ground coriander

- ✓ ¼ cup chopped fresh cilantro

Instructions

1. In a small bowl, whisk together the olive oil, rosemary, garlic, and salt. 2. Place the racks in a sealable freezer bag and pour the olive oil mixture into the bag. Massage the meat through the bag so it is coated with the marinade. Press the air out of the bag and seal it. 3. Marinate the lamb racks in the refrigerator for 1 to 2 hours. 4. Preheat the oven to 450°F. 5. Place a large ovenproof skillet over medium-high heat. Take the lamb racks out of the bag and sear them in the skillet on all sides, about 5 minutes in total. 6. Arrange the racks upright in the skillet, with the bones interlaced, and roast them in the oven until they reach your desired doneness, about 20 minutes for medium-rare or until the internal temperature reaches 125°F. 7. Let the lamb rest for 10 minutes and then cut the racks into chops. 8. Serve 4 chops per person.

Per Serving:

calories: 354 | fat: 30g | protein: 21g | carbs: 0g | net carbs: 0g | fiber: 0g

Balsamic Turkey Thighs

Preparation time: 5 minutes | Cook time: 1 hour | Serves 8

- ✓ ¼ cup (60 ml) balsamic vinegar
- ✓ ¼ cup (60 ml) refined avocado oil or refined olive oil
- ✓ 1 tablespoon Dijon mustard
- ✓ 2 teaspoons finely ground gray sea salt
- ✓ 1 teaspoon Italian seasoning

2½ pounds (Instructions

1.2 kg) bone-in, skin-on turkey thighs

Instructions

1. Place the vinegar, oil, mustard, salt, and seasoning in a large casserole dish or resealable plastic bag. Mix thoroughly. Add the turkey thighs and cover. Marinate in the refrigerator for 1 hour or up to 24 hours. 2. When ready to cook, preheat the oven to 350°F (177°C). Lay the turkey thighs on an unlined rimmed baking sheet or cast-iron pan. Bake for 55 to 60 minutes, until the internal temperature reaches

165°F (74°C) and the juices run clear. 3. Turn the oven broiler to high. (If your oven does not offer that option, simply "broil" is fine.) Broil for 3 to 5 minutes, until browned. Allow to rest for 5 minutes before slicing and serving.

Per Serving:

calories: 333 | fat: 25g | protein: 27g | carbs: 0g | net carbs: 0g | fiber: 0g

Ham Chicken with Cheese

Preparation time: 15 minutes | Cook time: 25 minutes | Serves 4

- ¼ cup unsalted butter, softened
- 4 ounces (113 g) cream cheese, softened
- 1½ teaspoons Dijon mustard
- 2 tablespoons white wine vinegar
- ¼ cup water
- 2 cups shredded cooked chicken
- ¼ pound (113 g) ham, chopped
- 4 ounces (113 g) sliced Swiss or Provolone cheese

Instructions

1. Preheat the air fryer to 380°F (193°C). Lightly coat a casserole dish that will fit in the air fryer, such as an 8-inch round pan, with olive oil and set aside. 2. In a large bowl and using an electric mixer, combine the butter, cream cheese, Dijon mustard, and vinegar. With the motor running at low speed, slowly add the water and beat until smooth. Set aside. 3. Arrange an even layer of chicken in the bottom of the prepared pan, followed by the ham. Spread the butter and cream cheese mixture on top of the ham, followed by the cheese slices on the top layer. Air fry for 20 to 25 minutes until warmed through and the cheese has browned.

Per Serving:

calories: 509 | fat: 39g | protein: 35g | carbs: 2g | net carbs: 2g | fiber: 0g

White Wine Seared Chicken Breasts

Preparation time: 10 minutes | Cook time: 30 minutes | Serves 4

- 4 medium boneless, skinless chicken breasts (8

ounces / 227 g each)
- 1 teaspoon sea salt
- ¼ teaspoon black pepper
- 4 tablespoons (½ stick) butter, cut into 1-tablespoon pats
- 2 cloves garlic, minced
- 1 medium shallot, finely chopped
- ½ cup white cooking wine
- ½ cup chicken broth
- ½ tablespoon chopped fresh parsley
- ½ tablespoon fresh thyme, chopped

Instructions

1. Season the chicken on both sides with sea salt and black pepper. 2. In a large skillet or sauté pan, melt 1 tablespoon of the butter over medium-high heat. Add the chicken and sauté for 5 to 8 minutes per side, until cooked through and browned. 3. Remove the chicken from the pan and cover with foil. 4. Add another 1 tablespoon butter to the pan. Add the garlic and shallot, and sauté for about 1 minute, until fragrant. 5. Add the wine and broth to the pan and use a wooden spoon to scrape any browned bits from the bottom. Bring to a gentle boil, then lower the heat and simmer for about 7 to 8 minutes, until the liquid volume is reduced by half. 6. Reduce the heat to low. Stir in the remaining 2 tablespoons butter, parsley, and thyme, just until the butter melts. 7. Serve the sauce over the chicken.

Per Serving:

calories: 288 | fat: 14g | protein: 29g | carbs: 2g | net carbs: 2g | fiber: 0g

Quattro Formaggi Chicken

Preparation time: 10 minutes | Cook time: 45 minutes | Serves 8

- 3 pounds chicken breasts
- 2 ounces mozzarella cheese, cubed
- 2 ounces mascarpone cheese
- 4 ounces cheddar cheese, cubed
- 2 ounces provolone cheese, cubed
- 1 zucchini, shredded
- Salt and ground black pepper, to taste
- 1 teaspoon garlic, minced

✓ ½ cup pancetta, cooked and crumbled

Instructions

1. Sprinkle black pepper and salt to the zucchini, squeeze well, and place to a bowl. Stir in the pancetta, mascarpone, cheddar cheese, provolone cheese, mozzarella, black pepper, and garlic. 2. Cut slits into chicken breasts, apply black pepper and salt, and stuff with the zucchini and cheese mixture. Set on a lined baking sheet, place in the oven at 400°F, and bake for 45 minutes.

Per Serving:

calories: 477 | fat: 24g | protein: 61g | carbs: 3g | net carbs: 2g | fiber: 1g

Butter and Bacon Chicken

Preparation time: 10 minutes | Cook time: 65 minutes | Serves 6

1 (4 pound / Instructions

1.8-kg) whole chicken

✓ 2 tablespoons salted butter, softened
✓ 1 teaspoon dried thyme
✓ ½ teaspoon garlic powder
✓ 1 teaspoon salt
✓ ½ teaspoon ground black pepper
✓ 6 slices sugar-free bacon

Instructions

1. Pat chicken dry with a paper towel, then rub with butter on all sides. Sprinkle thyme, garlic powder, salt, and pepper over chicken. 2. Place chicken into ungreased air fryer basket, breast side up. Lay strips of bacon over chicken and secure with toothpicks. 3. Adjust the temperature to 350°F (177°C) and air fry for 65 minutes. Halfway through cooking, remove and set aside bacon and flip chicken over. Chicken will be done when the skin is golden and crispy and the internal temperature is at least 165°F (74°C). Serve warm with bacon.

Per Serving:

calories: 563 | fat: 37g | protein: 56g | carbs: 1g | net carbs: 1g | fiber: 0g

Shredded Chicken

Preparation time: 5 minutes | Cook time: 14

minutes | Serves 4

✓ ½ teaspoon salt
✓ ½ teaspoon pepper
✓ ½ teaspoon dried oregano
✓ ½ teaspoon dried basil
✓ ½ teaspoon garlic powder
✓ 2 (6-ounce / 170-g) boneless, skinless chicken breasts
✓ 1 tablespoon coconut oil
✓ 1 cup water

Instructions

1. In a small bowl, combine the salt, pepper, oregano, basil, and garlic powder. Rub this mix over both sides of the chicken. 2. Set your Instant Pot to Sauté and heat the coconut oil until sizzling. 3. Add the chicken and sear for 3 to 4 minutes until golden on both sides. 4. Remove the chicken and set aside. 5. Pour the water into the Instant Pot and use a wooden spoon or rubber spatula to make sure no seasoning is stuck to bottom of pot. 6. Add the trivet to the Instant Pot and place the chicken on top. 7. Secure the lid. Select the Manual mode and set the cooking time for 10 minutes at High Pressure. 8. Once cooking is complete, do a natural pressure release for 5 minutes, then release any remaining pressure. Carefully open the lid. 9. Remove the chicken and shred, then serve.

Per Serving:

calories: 135 | fat: 5g | protein: 20g | carbs: 0g | net carbs: 0g | fiber: 0g

Turmeric Chicken Nuggets

Preparation time: 10 minutes | Cook time: 9 minutes | Serves 5

✓ 8 ounces (227 g) chicken fillet
✓ 1 teaspoon ground turmeric
✓ ½ teaspoon ground coriander
✓ ½ cup almond flour
✓ 2 eggs, beaten
✓ ½ cup butter

Instructions

1. Chop the chicken fillet roughly into the medium size pieces. 2. In the mixing bowl, mix up ground

turmeric, ground coriander, and almond flour. 3. Then dip the chicken pieces in the beaten egg and coat in the almond flour mixture. 4. Toss the butter in the instant pot and melt it on Sauté mode for 4 minutes. 5. Then put the coated chicken in the hot butter and cook for 5 minutes or until the nuggets are golden brown.

Per Serving:

calories: 343 | fat: 29g | protein: 18g | carbs: 3g | net carbs: 2g | fiber: 1g

Buffalo Chicken Wings

Preparation time: 10 minutes | Cook time: 20 to 25 minutes | Serves 4

- ✓ 2 tablespoons baking powder
- ✓ 1 teaspoon smoked paprika
- ✓ Sea salt and freshly ground black pepper, to taste
- ✓ 2 pounds (907 g) chicken wings or chicken drumettes
- ✓ Avocado oil spray
- ✓ ⅓ cup avocado oil
- ✓ ½ cup Buffalo hot sauce, such as Frank's RedHot
- ✓ ¼ cup (4 tablespoons) unsalted butter
- ✓ 2 tablespoons apple cider vinegar
- ✓ 1 teaspoon minced garlic

Instructions

1. In a large bowl, stir together the baking powder, smoked paprika, and salt and pepper to taste. Add the chicken wings and toss to coat. 2. Set the air fryer to 400°F (204°C). Spray the wings with oil. 3. Place the wings in the basket in a single layer, working in batches, and air fry for 20 to 25 minutes. Check with an instant-read thermometer and remove when they reach 155°F (68°C). Let rest until they reach 165°F (74°C). 4. While the wings are cooking, whisk together the avocado oil, hot sauce, butter, vinegar, and garlic in a small saucepan over medium-low heat until warm. 5. When the wings are done cooking, toss them with the Buffalo sauce. Serve warm.

Per Serving:

calories: 616 | fat: 52g | protein: 28g | carbs: 3g | net carbs: 3g | fiber: 0g

Curry Chicken Salad

Preparation time: 10 minutes | Cook time: 0 minutes | Serves 4

- ✓ 1½ pounds boneless, skinless chicken thighs, cooked
- ✓ ⅓ cup mayonnaise, homemade or store-bought
- ✓ 2 tablespoons sour cream
- ✓ Juice of ½ lemon
- ✓ 1½ tablespoons minced fresh chives, plus extra for garnish
- ✓ 1½ teaspoons curry powder
- ✓ ¼ teaspoon pink Himalayan salt
- ✓ ¼ teaspoon ground black pepper
- ✓ 2 stalks celery, chopped

Instructions

1. Chop the cooked chicken into bite-sized pieces and set aside. 2. Put the mayo, sour cream, lemon juice, chives, curry powder, salt, and pepper in a medium-sized mixing bowl and stir to combine. 3. Add the chicken pieces and celery to the mayo mixture and toss to coat thoroughly. Serve garnished with additional chives, if desired.

Per Serving:

calories: 339 | fat: 14g | protein: 25g | carbs: 2g | net carbs: 1g | fiber: 1g

CHAPTER 3 Beef, Pork, and Lamb

Garlic-Marinated Flank Steak

Preparation time: 30 minutes | Cook time: 8 to 10 minutes | Serves 6

- ✓ ½ cup avocado oil
- ✓ ¼ cup coconut aminos
- ✓ 1 shallot, minced
- ✓ 1 tablespoon minced garlic
- ✓ 2 tablespoons chopped fresh oregano, or 2 teaspoons dried
- ✓ 1½ teaspoons sea salt
- ✓ 1 teaspoon freshly ground black pepper
- ✓ ¼ teaspoon red pepper flakes
- ✓ 2 pounds (907 g) flank steak

Instructions

1. In a blender, combine the avocado oil, coconut aminos, shallot, garlic, oregano, salt, black pepper, and red pepper flakes. Process until smooth. 2. Place the steak in a zip-top plastic bag or shallow dish with the marinade. Seal the bag or cover the dish and marinate in the refrigerator for at least 2 hours or overnight. 3. Remove the steak from the bag and discard the marinade. 4. Set the air fryer to 400°F (204°C). Place the steak in the air fryer basket (if needed, cut into sections and work in batches). Air fry for 4 to 6 minutes, flip the steak, and cook for another 4 minutes or until the internal temperature reaches 120°F (49°C) in the thickest part for medium-rare (or as desired).

Per Serving:

calories: 360 | fat: 20g | protein: 38g | carbs: 4g | net carbs: 4g | fiber: 0g

Ground Beef Cabbage Casserole

Preparation time: 5 minutes | Cook time: 4 minutes | Serves 4

- ✓ 1 pound (454 g) 85% lean ground beef
- ✓ 2 cups shredded white cabbage

- ✓ 1 cup salsa
- ✓ 1 teaspoon salt
- ✓ 1 tablespoon chili powder
- ✓ ½ teaspoon cumin
- ✓ ½ cup water
- ✓ 1 cup shredded Cheddar cheese

Instructions

1. Press the Sauté button and brown ground beef. Once fully cooked, add remaining ingredients except for cheese. 2. Click lid closed. Press the Manual button and adjust timer for 4 minutes. When timer beeps, quick release the pressure and stir in Cheddar.

Per Serving:

calories: 393 | fat: 23g | protein: 30g | carbs: 5g | net carbs: 3g | fiber: 2g

Five-Spice Pork Belly

Preparation time: 10 minutes | Cook time: 17 minutes | Serves 4

- ✓ 1 pound (454 g) unsalted pork belly
- ✓ 2 teaspoons Chinese five-spice powder
- ✓ Sauce:
- ✓ 1 tablespoon coconut oil
- ✓ 1 (1-inch) piece fresh ginger, peeled and grated
- ✓ 2 cloves garlic, minced
- ✓ ½ cup beef or chicken broth
- ✓ ¼ to ½ cup Swerve confectioners'-style sweetener or equivalent amount of liquid or powdered sweetener
- ✓ 3 tablespoons wheat-free tamari, or ½ cup coconut aminos
- ✓ 1 green onion, sliced, plus more for garnish

Instructions

1. Spray the air fryer basket with avocado oil. Preheat the air fryer to 400°F (204°C). 2. Cut the pork belly into ½-inch-thick slices and season well on all sides

with the five-spice powder. Place the slices in a single layer in the air fryer basket (if you're using a smaller air fryer, work in batches if necessary) and cook for 8 minutes, or until cooked to your liking, flipping halfway through. 3. While the pork belly cooks, make the sauce: Heat the coconut oil in a small saucepan over medium heat. Add the ginger and garlic and sauté for 1 minute, or until fragrant. Add the broth, sweetener, and tamari and simmer for 10 to 15 minutes, until thickened. Add the green onion and cook for another minute, until the green onion is softened. Taste and adjust the seasoning to your liking. 4. Transfer the pork belly to a large bowl. Pour the sauce over the pork belly and coat well. Place the pork belly slices on a serving platter and garnish with sliced green onions. 5. Best served fresh. Store leftovers in an airtight container in the fridge for up to 4 days. Reheat in a preheated 400°F (204°C) air fryer for 3 minutes, or until heated through.

Per Serving:

calories: 533 | fat: 49g | protein: 14g | carbs: 6g | net carbs: 3g | fiber: 3g

Chili-Stuffed Avocados

Preparation time: 10 minutes | Cook time: 30 minutes | Serves 8

- ✓ 2 tablespoons tallow or bacon grease
- ✓ 1 pound (455 g) ground beef (20% to 30% fat)
- ✓ 1 (14½-ounce/408-g/428-ml) can whole tomatoes with juices
- ✓ 1½ tablespoons chili powder
- ✓ 2 small cloves garlic, minced
- ✓ 2 teaspoons paprika
- ✓ ¾ teaspoon finely ground gray sea salt
- ✓ ¼ teaspoon ground cinnamon
- ✓ 2 tablespoons finely chopped fresh parsley
- ✓ 4 large Hass avocados, sliced in half, pits removed (leave skin on), for serving

Instructions

1. Place the tallow into a large saucepan. Melt on medium heat before adding the ground beef. Cook until beef is no longer pink, 7 to 8 minutes, stirring often to break the meat up into small clumps. 2. Add the tomatoes, chili powder, garlic, paprika, salt, and cinnamon. Cover and bring to a boil on high heat. Once boiling, reduce the heat to medium-low and simmer for 20 to 25 minutes, with the cover slightly askew to let steam out. 3. Once thickened, remove from the heat and stir in the chopped parsley. 4. Place an avocado half on a small serving plate or on a platter if you plan to serve them family style. Scoop ⅓ scant cup (180g) of chili into the hollow of

Per Serving:

calories: 385 | fat: 31g | protein: 17g | carbs: 10g | net carbs: 3g | fiber: 7g

Osso Buco with Gremolata

Preparation time: 35 minutes | Cook time: 1 hour 2 minutes | Serves 6

- ✓ 4 bone-in beef shanks
- ✓ Sea salt, to taste
- ✓ 2 tablespoons avocado oil
- ✓ 1 small turnip, diced
- ✓ 1 medium onion, diced
- ✓ 1 medium stalk celery, diced
- ✓ 4 cloves garlic, smashed
- ✓ 1 tablespoon unsweetened tomato purée
- ✓ ½ cup dry white wine
- ✓ 1 cup chicken broth
- ✓ 1 sprig fresh rosemary
- ✓ 2 sprigs fresh thyme
- ✓ 3 Roma tomatoes, diced
- ✓ For the Gremolata:
- ✓ ½ cup loosely packed parsley leaves
- ✓ 1 clove garlic, crushed
- ✓ Grated zest of 2 lemons

Instructions

1. On a clean work surface, season the shanks all over with salt. 2. Set the Instant Pot to Sauté and add the oil. When the oil shimmers, add 2 shanks and sear for 4 minutes per side. Remove the shanks to a bowl and repeat with the remaining shanks. Set aside. 3. Add the turnip, onion, and celery to the pot and cook for 5 minutes or until softened. 4. Add the garlic and unsweetened tomato purée and cook 1 minute more,

stirring frequently. 5. Deglaze the pot with the wine, scraping the bottom with a wooden spoon to loosen any browned bits. Bring to a boil. 6. Add the broth, rosemary, thyme, and shanks, then add the tomatoes on top of the shanks. 7. Secure the lid. Press the Manual button and set cooking time for 40 minutes on High Pressure. 8. Meanwhile, for the gremolata: In a small food processor, combine the parsley, garlic, and lemon zest and pulse until the parsley is finely chopped. Refrigerate until ready to use. 9. When timer beeps, allow the pressure to release naturally for 20 minutes, then release any remaining pressure. Open the lid. 10. To serve, transfer the shanks to large, shallow serving bowl. Ladle the braising sauce over the top and sprinkle with the gremolata.

Per Serving:

calories: 605 | fat: 30g | protein: 69g | carbs: 8g | net carbs: 6g | fiber: 2g

Sausage-Stuffed Peppers

Preparation time: 15 minutes | Cook time: 28 to 30 minutes | Serves 6

- ✓ Avocado oil spray
- ✓ 8 ounces (227 g) Italian sausage, casings removed
- ✓ ½ cup chopped mushrooms
- ✓ ¼ cup diced onion
- ✓ 1 teaspoon Italian seasoning
- ✓ Sea salt and freshly ground black pepper, to taste
- ✓ 1 cup keto-friendly marinara sauce
- ✓ 3 bell peppers, halved and seeded
- ✓ 3 ounces (85 g) provolone cheese, shredded

Instructions

1. Spray a large skillet with oil and place it over medium-high heat. Add the sausage and cook for 5 minutes, breaking up the meat with a wooden spoon. Add the mushrooms, onion, and Italian seasoning, and season with salt and pepper. Cook for 5 minutes more. Stir in the marinara sauce and cook until heated through. 2. Scoop the sausage filling into the bell pepper halves. 3. Set the air fryer to 350°F (177°C). Arrange the peppers in a single layer in the air fryer basket, working in batches if necessary. Air fry for 15 minutes. 4. Top the stuffed peppers with the cheese and air fry for 3 to 5 minutes more, until the cheese is melted and the peppers are tender.

Per Serving:

calories: 205 | fat: 16g | protein: 10g | carbs: 6g | net carbs: 5g | fiber: 1g

Sweet Beef Curry

Preparation time: 10 minutes | Cook time: 30 minutes | Serves 4

- ✓ ½ cup (105 g) coconut oil, or ½ cup (120 ml) avocado oil
- ✓ 1 small apple, peeled, cored, and diced
- ✓ 1 small yellow onion, sliced
- ✓ 2 cloves garlic, minced
- ✓ 1 (3-in/7.5-cm) piece fresh ginger root, minced
- ✓ 2 tablespoons curry powder
- ✓ 2 teaspoons garam masala
- ✓ 1 pound (455 g) boneless beef chuck roast, cut into ¾-inch (2-cm) cubes
- ✓ 1 small butternut squash (about 1 lb/455 g), cubed
- ✓ 1 cup (240 ml) beef bone broth
- ✓ 1 tablespoon coconut aminos

Instructions

1. Heat the oil in a large saucepan over medium heat. Add the apple, onion, garlic, ginger, curry powder, and garam masala and toss to coat. Sauté for 10 minutes, or until fragrant. 2. Add the beef, squash, broth, and coconut aminos. Cover and bring to a boil over high heat. Reduce the heat to medium-low and simmer for 20 minutes, until the squash is fork-tender to soft. 3. Divide the curry among 4 bowls and enjoy.

Per Serving:

calories: 698 | fat: 56g | protein: 32g | carbs: 17g | net carbs: 13g | fiber: 4g

Spinach Feta Stuffed Pork

Preparation time: 15 minutes | Cook time: 30 minutes | Serves 4

- ✓ 4 ounces crumbled feta cheese

- ✓ ¾ cup chopped frozen spinach, thawed and liquid squeezed out
- ✓ 3 tablespoons chopped Kalamata olives
- ✓ 4 (4-ounce) center pork chops, 2 inches thick
- ✓ Sea salt, for seasoning
- ✓ Freshly ground black pepper, for seasoning
- ✓ 3 tablespoons good-quality olive oil

Instructions

1. Preheat the oven. Set the oven temperature to 400°F. 2. Make the filling. In a small bowl, mix together the feta, spinach, and olives until everything is well combined. 3. Stuff the pork chops. Make a horizontal slit in the side of each chop to create a pocket, making sure you don't cut all the way through. Stuff the filling equally between the chops and secure the slits with toothpicks. Lightly season the stuffed chops with salt and pepper. 4. Brown the chops. In a large oven-safe skillet over medium-high heat, warm the olive oil. Add the chops and sear them until they're browned all over, about 10 minutes in total. 5. Roast the chops. Place the skillet in the oven and roast the chops for 20 minutes or until they're cooked through. 6. Serve. Let the meat rest for 10 minutes and then remove the toothpicks. Divide the pork chops between four plates and serve them immediately.

Per Serving:

calories: 342 | fat: 24g | protein: 28g | carbs: 3g | net carbs: 2g | fiber: 1g

Deconstructed Egg Rolls

Preparation time: 10 minutes | Cook time: 15 minutes | Serves 6

- ✓ 1 pound (454 g) ground pork
- ✓ 1 tablespoon untoasted, cold-pressed sesame oil
- ✓ 6 cups finely shredded cabbage
- ✓ 2 teaspoons minced garlic
- ✓ 1 tablespoon minced fresh ginger
- ✓ 1 tablespoon coconut aminos or wheat-free tamari
- ✓ 1 teaspoon fish sauce (optional)
- ✓ ¼ cup chopped green onions, for garnish

Instructions

1. Place the pork and oil in a large cast-iron skillet over medium-high heat and cook, crumbling the meat with a wooden spoon, until cooked through, about 10 minutes. (Do not drain the drippings from the pan.) 2. Add the cabbage, garlic, ginger, coconut aminos, and fish sauce, if using, to the skillet. Sauté until the cabbage is soft, 3 to 5 minutes. 3. Divide among six plates or bowls and serve garnished with the green onions.

Per Serving:

calories: 250 | fat: 19g | protein: 14g | carbs: 6g | net carbs: 3g | fiber: 3g

Deconstructed Chicago Dogs

Preparation time: 10 minutes | Cook time: 7 minutes | Serves 4

- ✓ 4 hot dogs
- ✓ 2 large dill pickles
- ✓ ¼ cup diced onions
- ✓ 1 tomato, cut into ½-inch dice
- ✓ 4 pickled sport peppers, diced
- ✓ For Garnish (Optional):
- ✓ Brown mustard
- ✓ Celery salt
- ✓ Poppy seeds

Instructions

1. Spray the air fryer basket with avocado oil. Preheat the air fryer to 400°F (204°C). 2. Place the hot dogs in the air fryer basket and air fry for 5 to 7 minutes, until hot and slightly crispy. 3. While the hot dogs cook, quarter one of the dill pickles lengthwise, so that you have 4 pickle spears. Finely dice the other pickle. 4. When the hot dogs are done, transfer them to a serving platter and arrange them in a row, alternating with the pickle spears. Top with the diced pickles, onions, tomato, and sport peppers. Drizzle brown mustard on top and garnish with celery salt and poppy seeds, if desired. 5. Best served fresh. Store leftover hot dogs in an airtight container in the refrigerator for up to 3 days. Reheat in a preheated 390°F (199°C) air fryer for 2 minutes, or until warmed through.

Per Serving:

calories: 208 | fat: 16g | protein: 8g | carbs: 9g | net carbs: 6g | fiber: 3g

Beef Shami Kabob

Preparation time: 15 minutes | Cook time: 35 minutes | Serves 4

- ✓ 1 pound (454 g) beef chunks, chopped
- ✓ 1 teaspoon ginger paste
- ✓ ½ teaspoon ground cumin
- ✓ 2 cups water
- ✓ ¼ cup almond flour
- ✓ 1 egg, beaten
- ✓ 1 tablespoon coconut oil

Instructions

1. Put the beef chunks, ginger paste, ground cumin, and water in the Instant Pot. 2. Select Manual mode and set cooking time for 30 minutes on High Pressure. 3. When timer beeps, make a quick pressure release. Open the lid. 4. Drain the water from the meat. Transfer the beef in the blender. Add the almond flour and beaten egg. Blend until smooth. Shape the mixture into small meatballs. 5. Heat the coconut oil on Sauté mode and put the meatballs inside. 6. Cook for 2 minutes on each side or until golden brown. 7. Serve immediately.

Per Serving:

calories: 179 | fat: 10g | protein: 20g | carbs: 3g | net carbs: 3g | fiber: 0g

Lamb Kofte with Yogurt Sauce

Preparation time: 30 minutes | Cook time: 15 minutes | Serves 4

- ✓ 1 pound (454 g) ground lamb
- ✓ ½ cup finely chopped fresh mint, plus 2 tablespoons
- ✓ ¼ cup almond or coconut flour
- ✓ ¼ cup finely chopped red onion
- ✓ ¼ cup toasted pine nuts
- ✓ 2 teaspoons ground cumin
- ✓ 1½ teaspoons salt, divided
- ✓ 1 teaspoon ground cinnamon
- ✓ 1 teaspoon ground ginger
- ✓ ½ teaspoon ground nutmeg
- ✓ ½ teaspoon freshly ground black pepper
- ✓ 1 cup plain whole-milk Greek yogurt
- ✓ 2 tablespoons extra-virgin olive oil
- ✓ Zest and juice of 1 lime

Instructions

1. Heat the oven broiler to the low setting. You can also bake these at high heat (450 to 475°F/ 235 to 245°C) if you happen to have a very hot broiler. Submerge four wooden skewers in water and let soak at least 10 minutes to prevent them from burning. 2. In a large bowl, combine the lamb, ½ cup mint, almond flour, red onion, pine nuts, cumin, 1 teaspoon salt, cinnamon, ginger, nutmeg, and pepper and, using your hands, incorporate all the ingredients together well. 3. Form the mixture into 12 egg-shaped patties and let sit for 10 minutes. 4. Remove the skewers from the water, thread 3 patties onto each skewer, and place on a broiling pan or wire rack on top of a baking sheet lined with aluminum foil. Broil on the top rack until golden and cooked through, 8 to 12 minutes, flipping once halfway through cooking. 5. While the meat cooks, in a small bowl, combine the yogurt, olive oil, remaining 2 tablespoons chopped mint, remaining ½ teaspoon salt, and lime zest and juice and whisk to combine well. Keep cool until ready to use. 6. Serve the skewers with yogurt sauce.

Per Serving:

calories: 592 | fat: 46g | protein: 28g | carbs: 12g | net carbs: 8g | fiber: 4g

Barbacoa Beef Roast

Preparation time: 10 minutes | Cook time: 8 hours | Serves 2

- ✓ 1 pound beef chuck roast
- ✓ Pink Himalayan salt
- ✓ Freshly ground black pepper
- ✓ 4 chipotle peppers in adobo sauce (I use La Costeña 12-ounce can)
- ✓ 1 (6-ounce) can green jalapeño chiles
- ✓ 2 tablespoons apple cider vinegar
- ✓ ½ cup beef broth

Instructions

1. With the crock insert in place, preheat the slow cooker to low. 2. Season the beef chuck roast on both sides with pink Himalayan salt and pepper. Put the roast in the slow cooker. 3. In a food processor (or blender), combine the chipotle peppers and their adobo sauce, jalapeños, and apple cider vinegar, and pulse until smooth. Add the beef broth, and pulse a few more times. Pour the chile mixture over the top of the roast. 4. Cover and cook on low for 8 hours. 5. Transfer the beef to a cutting board, and use two forks to shred the meat. 6. Serve hot.

Per Serving:

calories: 723 | fat: 46g | protein: 66g | carbs: 7g | net carbs: 2g | fiber: 5g

North African Lamb

Preparation time: 10 minutes | Cook time: 10 minutes | Serves 4

- ✓ 2 teaspoons paprika
- ✓ 2 garlic cloves, minced
- ✓ 2 teaspoons dried oregano
- ✓ 2 tablespoons sumac
- ✓ 12 lamb cutlets
- ✓ ¼ cup sesame oil
- ✓ 2 teaspoons cumin
- ✓ 4 carrots, sliced
- ✓ ¼ cup fresh parsley, chopped
- ✓ 2 teaspoons harissa paste
- ✓ 1 tablespoon red wine vinegar
- ✓ Salt and black pepper, to taste
- ✓ 2 tablespoons black olives, sliced
- ✓ 2 cucumbers, sliced

Instructions

1. In a bowl, combine the cutlets with the paprika, oregano, black pepper, 2 tablespoons water, half of the oil, sumac, garlic, and salt, and rub well. Add the carrots in a pot, cover with water, bring to a boil over medium heat, cook for 2 minutes then drain before placing them in a salad bowl. 2. Place the cucumbers and olives to the carrots. In another bowl, combine the harissa with the rest of the oil, a splash of water, parsley, vinegar, and cumin. Place this to the carrots mixture, season with pepper and salt, and toss well

to coat. 3. Preheat the grill to medium heat and arrange the lamb cutlets on it, grill each side for 3 minutes, and split among separate plates. Serve alongside the carrot salad.

Per Serving:

calories: 354 | fat: 23g | protein: 27g | carbs: 7g | net carbs: 4g | fiber: 3g

Cottage Pie

Preparation time: 20 minutes | Cook time: 30 minutes | Serves 4

- ✓ Pie:
- ✓ 2 tablespoons extra-virgin olive oil
- ✓ 2 celery stalks, chopped
- ✓ ½ medium onion, chopped
- ✓ 2 garlic cloves, minced
- ✓ 1 pound (454 g) ground beef
- ✓ ¼ cup chicken broth
- ✓ 1 tablespoon tomato paste
- ✓ 1 teaspoon pink Himalayan sea salt
- ✓ 1 teaspoon freshly ground black pepper
- ✓ ½ teaspoon ground white pepper
- ✓ Topping:
- ✓ 2 (12-ounce / 340-g) packages cauliflower rice, cooked and drained
- ✓ 1 cup shredded low-moisture mozzarella cheese
- ✓ 2 tablespoons heavy (whipping) cream
- ✓ 2 tablespoons butter
- ✓ ½ teaspoon pink Himalayan sea salt
- ✓ ½ teaspoon freshly ground black pepper
- ✓ ¼ teaspoon ground white pepper
- ✓ ¼ teaspoon garlic powder

Instructions

1. Preheat the oven to 400°F (205°C). 2. To make the pie: In a large sauté pan or skillet, heat the olive oil over medium heat. Add the celery and onion and cook for 8 to 10 minutes, until the onion is tender. 3. Add the garlic and cook for an additional minute, until fragrant. 4. Add the ground beef, breaking it up with a wooden spoon or spatula. Continue to cook the beef for 7 to 10 minutes, until fully browned. 5. Stir in the broth and tomato paste and stir to coat the meat. Sprinkle in the salt, black pepper, and white

pepper. 6. Transfer the meat mixture to a 9-by-13-inch baking dish. 7. To make the topping: In a food processor, combine the cauliflower rice, mozzarella, cream, butter, salt, black pepper, white pepper, and garlic powder. Purée on high speed until the mixture is smooth, scraping down the sides of the bowl as necessary. 8. Spread the cauliflower mash over the top of the meat and smooth the top. 9. Bake for 10 minutes, until the topping is just lightly browned. Let cool for 5 minutes, then serve.

Per Serving:

calories: 564 | fat: 44g | protein: 30g | carbs: 13g | net carbs: 7g | fiber: 6g

Blue Pork

Preparation time: 5 minutes | Cook time: 20 minutes | Serves 2

- ✓ 1 teaspoon coconut oil
- ✓ 2 pork chops
- ✓ 2 ounces (57 g) blue cheese, crumbled
- ✓ 1 teaspoon lemon juice
- ✓ ¼ cup heavy cream

Instructions

1. Heat the coconut oil in the Instant Pot on Sauté mode. 2. Put the pork chops in the Instant Pot and cook on Sauté mode for 5 minutes on each side. 3. Add the lemon juice and crumbled cheese. Stir to mix well. 4. Add heavy cream and close the lid. 5. Select Manual mode and set cooking time for 10 minutes on High Pressure. 6. When timer beeps, perform a natural pressure release for 5 minutes, then release any remaining pressure. Open the lid. 7. Serve immediately.

Per Serving:

calories: 300 | fat: 26g | protein: 15g | carbs: 1g | net carbs: 1g | fiber: 0g

Herbed Lamb Steaks

Preparation time: 30 minutes | Cook time: 15 minutes | Serves 4

- ✓ ½ medium onion
- ✓ 2 tablespoons minced garlic
- ✓ 2 teaspoons ground ginger

- ✓ 1 teaspoon ground cinnamon
- ✓ 1 teaspoon onion powder
- ✓ 1 teaspoon cayenne pepper
- ✓ 1 teaspoon salt
- ✓ 4 (6 ounces / 170 g) boneless lamb sirloin steaks
- ✓ Oil, for spraying

Instructions

1. In a blender, combine the onion, garlic, ginger, cinnamon, onion powder, cayenne pepper, and salt and pulse until the onion is minced. 2. Place the lamb steaks in a large bowl or zip-top plastic bag and sprinkle the onion mixture over the top. Turn the steaks until they are evenly coated. Cover with plastic wrap or seal the bag and refrigerate for 30 minutes. 3. Preheat the air fryer to 330°F (166°C). Line the air fryer basket with parchment and spray lightly with oil. 4. Place the lamb steaks in a single layer in the prepared basket, making sure they don't overlap. You may need to work in batches, depending on the size of your air fryer. 5. Cook for 8 minutes, flip, and cook for another 7 minutes, or until the internal temperature reaches 155°F (68°C).

Per Serving:

calories: 206 | fat: 10g | protein: 26g | carbs: 6g | net carbs: 4g | fiber: 2g

Garlic Balsamic London Broil

Preparation time: 30 minutes | Cook time: 8 to 10 minutes | Serves 8

- ✓ 2 pounds (907 g) London broil
- ✓ 3 large garlic cloves, minced
- ✓ 3 tablespoons balsamic vinegar
- ✓ 3 tablespoons whole-grain mustard
- ✓ 2 tablespoons olive oil
- ✓ Sea salt and ground black pepper, to taste
- ✓ ½ teaspoon dried hot red pepper flakes

Instructions

1. Score both sides of the cleaned London broil. 2. Thoroughly combine the remaining ingredients; massage this mixture into the meat to coat it on all sides. Let it marinate for at least 3 hours. 3. Set the air fryer to 400°F (204°C); Then cook the London

broil for 15 minutes. Flip it over and cook another 10 to 12 minutes. Bon appétit!

Per Serving:

calories: 285 | fat: 13g | protein: 37g | carbs: 2g | net carbs: 2g | fiber: 0g

Romano-Crusted Pork Chops

Preparation time: 10 minutes | Cook time: 18 minutes | Serves 3

- ✓ 3 pork chops
- ✓ 4 ounces (113 g) Romano cheese, grated
- ✓ ½ teaspoon Cajun seasoning
- ✓ 1 egg, beaten
- ✓ 1 tablespoon cream cheese
- ✓ ⅓ cup almond flour
- ✓ 3 tablespoons avocado oil

Instructions

1. Rub the pork chops with Cajun seasoning. 2. After this, in the mixing bowl mix up grated Romano cheese and almond flour. 3. In the separated bow mix up eggs and cream cheese. 4. Dip the pork chops in the egg mixture and then coat in the cheese mixture. 5. Repeat the step one more time. 6. Pour avocado oil in the instant pot. Preheat it on Sauté mode for 2 minutes. 7. Add the pork chops and cook them for 8 minutes per side.

Per Serving:

calories: 528 | fat: 40g | protein: 35g | carbs: 5g | net carbs: 3g | fiber: 2g

Beef and Butternut Squash Stew

Preparation time: 10 minutes | Cook time: 40 minutes | Serves 4

- ✓ 3 teaspoons olive oil
- ✓ 1 pound ground beef
- ✓ 1 cup beef stock
- ✓ 14 ounces canned tomatoes with juice
- ✓ 1 tablespoon stevia
- ✓ 1 pound butternut squash, chopped
- ✓ 1 tablespoon Worcestershire sauce
- ✓ 2 bay leaves
- ✓ Salt and black pepper, to taste
- ✓ 1 onion, chopped
- ✓ 1 teaspoon dried sage
- ✓ 1 tablespoon garlic, minced

Instructions

1. Set a pan over medium heat and heat olive oil, stir in the onion, garlic, and beef, and cook for 10 minutes. Add in butternut squash, Worcestershire sauce, bay leaves, stevia, beef stock, canned tomatoes, and sage, and bring to a boil. Reduce heat, and simmer for 30 minutes. 2. Remove and discard the bay leaves and adjust the seasonings. Split into bowls and enjoy.

Per Serving:

calories: 422 | fat: 21g | protein: 29g | carbs: 30g | net carbs: 23g | fiber: 7g

Mississippi Pot Roast

Preparation time: 5 minutes | Cook time: 8 minutes | Serves 4

- ✓ 1 pound beef chuck roast
- ✓ Pink Himalayan salt
- ✓ Freshly ground black pepper
- ✓ 1 (1-ounce) packet dry Au Jus Gravy Mix
- ✓ 1 (1-ounce) packet dry ranch dressing
- ✓ 8 tablespoons butter (1 stick)
- ✓ 1 cup whole pepperoncini (I use Mezzetta)

Instructions

1. With the crock insert in place, preheat the slow cooker to low. 2. Season both sides of the beef chuck roast with pink Himalayan salt and pepper. Put in the slow cooker. 3. Sprinkle the gravy mix and ranch dressing packets on top of the roast. 4. Place the butter on top of the roast, and sprinkle the pepperoncini around it. 5. Cover and cook on low for 8 hours. 6. Shred the beef using two forks, and serve hot.

Per Serving:

calories: 504 | fat: 34g | protein: 36g | carbs: 6g | net carbs: 6g | fiber: 0g

Steak with Bell Pepper

Preparation time: 30 minutes | Cook time: 20 to 23 minutes | Serves 6

- ✓ ¼ cup avocado oil

- ✓ ¼ cup freshly squeezed lime juice
- ✓ 2 teaspoons minced garlic
- ✓ 1 tablespoon chili powder
- ✓ ½ teaspoon ground cumin
- ✓ Sea salt and freshly ground black pepper, to taste
- ✓ 1 pound (454 g) top sirloin steak or flank steak, thinly sliced against the grain
- ✓ 1 red bell pepper, cored, seeded, and cut into ½-inch slices
- ✓ 1 green bell pepper, cored, seeded, and cut into ½-inch slices
- ✓ 1 large onion, sliced

Instructions

1. In a small bowl or blender, combine the avocado oil, lime juice, garlic, chili powder, cumin, and salt and pepper to taste. 2. Place the sliced steak in a zip-top bag or shallow dish. Place the bell peppers and onion in a separate zip-top bag or dish. Pour half the marinade over the steak and the other half over the vegetables. Seal both bags and let the steak and vegetables marinate in the refrigerator for at least 1 hour or up to 4 hours. 3. Line the air fryer basket with an air fryer liner or aluminum foil. Remove the vegetables from their bag or dish and shake off any excess marinade. Set the air fryer to 400°F (204°C). Place the vegetables in the air fryer basket and cook for 13 minutes. 4. Remove the steak from its bag or dish and shake off any excess marinade. Place the steak on top of the vegetables in the air fryer, and cook for 7 to 10 minutes or until an instant-read thermometer reads 120°F (49°C) for medium-rare (or cook to your desired doneness). 5. Serve with desired fixings, such as keto tortillas, lettuce, sour cream, avocado slices, shredded Cheddar cheese, and cilantro.

Per Serving:

calories: 235 | fat: 15g | protein: 18g | carbs: 9g | net carbs: 6g | fiber: 3g

Zucchini Rolls

Preparation time: 10 minutes | Cook time: 0 minutes | Serves 4

- ✓ Rolls:
- ✓ 1 medium zucchini (about 7 ounces/200 g)
- ✓ 1 cup (120 g) cooked beef strips
- ✓ 5 medium radishes, sliced thin
- ✓ Dipping Sauce:
- ✓ ¼ cup (60 ml) extra-virgin olive oil or refined avocado oil
- ✓ 2 tablespoons hot sauce
- ✓ 2 teaspoons fresh lime juice

Instructions

1. Place the zucchini on a cutting board and, using a vegetable peeler, peel long strips from the zucchini until it is next to impossible to create a full, long strip. 2. Place a zucchini strip on a cutting board, with a short end facing you. Place a couple of pieces of beef and 3 or 4 radish slices at the short end closest to you. Roll it up, then stab with a toothpick to secure. Repeat with the remaining zucchini strips, placing the completed rolls on a serving plate. 3. In a small serving dish, whisk together the dipping sauce ingredients. Serve the dipping sauce alongside the rolls.

Per Serving:

calories: 370 | fat: 33g | protein: 14g | carbs: 4g | net carbs: 3g | fiber: 1g

Pork Meatballs

Preparation time: 10 minutes | Cook time: 12 minutes | Makes 18 meatballs

- ✓ 1 pound (454 g) ground pork
- ✓ 1 large egg, whisked
- ✓ ½ teaspoon garlic powder
- ✓ ½ teaspoon salt
- ✓ ½ teaspoon ground ginger
- ✓ ¼ teaspoon crushed red pepper flakes
- ✓ 1 medium scallion, trimmed and sliced

Instructions

1. Combine all ingredients in a large bowl. Spoon out 2 tablespoons mixture and roll into a ball. Repeat to form eighteen meatballs total. 2. Place meatballs into ungreased air fryer basket. Adjust the temperature to 400°F (204°C) and air fry for 12 minutes, shaking the basket three times throughout cooking.

Meatballs will be browned and have an internal temperature of at least 145°F (63°C) when done. Serve warm.

Per Serving:

calories: 77 | fat: 5g | protein: 7g | carbs: 0g | net carbs: 0g | fiber: 0g

Beef Bourguignon

Preparation time: 10 minutes | Cook time: 1 hour | Serves 4

- ✓ 3 tablespoons coconut oil
- ✓ 1 tablespoon dried parsley flakes
- ✓ 1 cup red wine
- ✓ 1 teaspoon dried thyme
- ✓ Salt and black pepper, to taste
- ✓ 1 bay leaf
- ✓ ⅓ cup coconut flour
- ✓ 2 pounds beef, cubed
- ✓ 12 small white onions
- ✓ 4 pancetta slices, chopped
- ✓ 2 garlic cloves, minced
- ✓ ½ pound mushrooms, chopped

Instructions

1. In a bowl, combine the wine with bay leaf, olive oil, thyme, pepper, parsley, salt, and the beef cubes; set aside for 3 hours. Drain the meat, and reserve the marinade. Toss the flour over the meat to coat. 2. Heat a pan over medium heat, stir in the pancetta, and cook until slightly browned. Place in the onions and garlic, and cook for 3 minutes. Stir-fry in the meat and mushrooms for 4-5 minutes. 3. Pour in the marinade and 1 cup of water; cover and cook for 50 minutes. Season to taste and serve.

Per Serving:

calories: 728 | fat: 47g | protein: 53g | carbs: 21g | net carbs: 14g | fiber: 7g

Grilled Herbed Pork Kebabs

Preparation time: 10 minutes | Cook time: 15 minutes | Serves 4

- ✓ ¼ cup good-quality olive oil
- ✓ 1 tablespoon minced garlic
- ✓ 2 teaspoons dried oregano
- ✓ 1 teaspoon dried basil
- ✓ 1 teaspoon dried parsley
- ✓ ½ teaspoon sea salt
- ✓ ¼ teaspoon freshly ground black pepper
- ✓ 1 (1-pound) pork tenderloin, cut into 1½-inch pieces

Instructions

1. Marinate the pork. In a medium bowl, stir together the olive oil, garlic, oregano, basil, parsley, salt, and pepper. Add the pork pieces and toss to coat them in the marinade. Cover the bowl and place it in the refrigerator for 2 to 4 hours. 2. Make the kebabs. Divide the pork pieces between four skewers, making sure to not crowd the meat. 3. Grill the kebabs. Preheat your grill to medium-high heat. Grill the skewers for about 12 minutes, turning to cook all sides of the pork, until the pork is cooked through. 4. Serve. Rest the skewers for 5 minutes. Divide the skewers between four plates and serve them immediately.

Per Serving:

calories: 261 | fat: 18g | protein: 24g | carbs: 1g | net carbs: 1g | fiber: 0g

Beef and Red Cabbage Stew

Preparation time: 10 minutes | Cook time: 20 minutes | Serves 4

- ✓ 2 tablespoons butter, at room temperature
- ✓ 1 onion, chopped
- ✓ 2 garlic cloves, minced
- ✓ 1½ pounds (680 g) beef stew meat, cubed
- ✓ 2½ cups beef stock
- ✓ 8 ounces (227 g) sugar-free tomato sauce
- ✓ 2 cups shredded red cabbage
- ✓ 1 tablespoon coconut aminos
- ✓ 2 bay leaves
- ✓ 1 teaspoon dried parsley flakes
- ✓ ½ teaspoon crushed red pepper flakes
- ✓ Sea salt and ground black pepper, to taste

Instructions

1. Press the Sauté button to heat up the Instant Pot. Then, melt the butter. Cook the onion and garlic until softened. 2. Add beef stew meat and cook an

additional 3 minutes or until browned. Stir the remaining ingredients into the Instant Pot. 3. Secure the lid. Choose Manual mode and High Pressure; cook for 15 minutes. Once cooking is complete, use a quick pressure release; carefully remove the lid. 4. Discard bay leaves and ladle into individual bowls. Enjoy!

Per Serving:

calories: 320 | fat: 16g | protein: 39g | carbs: 7g | net carbs: 5g | fiber: 2g

Pork Taco Casserole

Preparation time: 15 minutes | Cook time: 30 minutes | Serves 6

- ✓ ½ cup water
- ✓ 2 eggs
- ✓ 3 ounces (85 g) Cottage cheese, at room temperature
- ✓ ¼ cup heavy cream
- ✓ 1 teaspoon taco seasoning
- ✓ 6 ounces (170 g) Cotija cheese, crumbled
- ✓ ¾ pound (340 g) ground pork
- ✓ ½ cup tomatoes, puréed
- ✓ 1 tablespoon taco seasoning
- ✓ 3 ounces (85 g) chopped green chilies
- ✓ 6 ounces (170 g) Queso Manchego cheese, shredded

Instructions

1. Add the water in the Instant Pot and place in the trivet. 2. In a mixing bowl, combine the eggs, Cottage cheese, heavy cream, and taco seasoning. 3. Lightly grease a casserole dish. Spread the Cotija cheese over the bottom. Stir in the egg mixture. 4. Lower the casserole dish onto the trivet. 5. Secure the lid. Choose Manual mode and set cooking time for 20 minutes on High Pressure. 6. Once cooking is complete, use a quick pressure release. Carefully remove the lid. 7. In the meantime, heat a skillet over a medium-high heat. Brown the ground pork, crumbling with a fork. 8. Add the tomato purée, taco seasoning, and green chilies. Spread the mixture over the prepared cheese crust. 9. Top with shredded Queso Manchego. 10. Secure the lid. Choose Manual

mode and set cooking time for 10 minutes on High Pressure. 1Instructions

1. Once cooking is complete, use a quick pressure release. Carefully remove the lid. Serve immediately.

Per Serving:

calories: 409 | fat: 32g | protein: 26g | carbs: 5g | net carbs: 3g | fiber: 2g

Pork in White Wine

Preparation time: 15 minutes | Cook time: 1 hour 10 minutes | Serves 6

- ✓ 2 tablespoons olive oil
- ✓ 2 pounds pork stew meat, cubed
- ✓ Salt and black pepper, to taste
- ✓ 2 tablespoons butter
- ✓ 4 garlic cloves, minced
- ✓ ¾ cup vegetable stock
- ✓ ½ cup white wine
- ✓ 3 carrots, chopped
- ✓ 1 cabbage head, shredded
- ✓ ½ cup scallions, chopped
- ✓ 1cup heavy cream

Instructions

1. Set a pan over medium heat and warm butter and oil. Sear the pork until brown. Add garlic, scallions and carrots; sauté for 5 minutes. Pour in the cabbage, stock and wine, and bring to a boil. Reduce the heat and cook for 1 hour covered. Add in heavy cream as you stir for 1 minute, adjust seasonings and serve.

Per Serving:

calories: 673 | fat: 54g | protein: 29g | carbs: 17g | net carbs: 12g | fiber: 5g

Beef Zucchini Boats

Preparation time: 10 minutes | Cook time: 33 minutes | Serves 4

- ✓ 2 garlic cloves, minced
- ✓ 1 teaspoon cumin
- ✓ 1 tablespoon olive oil
- ✓ 1 pound ground beef
- ✓ ½ cup onions, chopped
- ✓ 1 teaspoon smoked paprika
- ✓ Salt and black pepper, to taste

- ✓ 4 zucchinis
- ✓ ¼ cup fresh cilantro, chopped
- ✓ ½ cup Monterey Jack cheese, shredded
- ✓ 1½ cups enchilada sauce
- ✓ 1 avocado, chopped, for serving
- ✓ Green onions, chopped, for serving
- ✓ Tomatoes, chopped, for serving

Instructions

1. Set a pan over high heat and warm the oil. Add the onions, and cook for 2 minutes. Stir in the beef, and brown for 4-5 minutes. Stir in the paprika, pepper, garlic, cumin, and salt; cook for 2 minutes. 2. Slice the zucchini in half lengthwise and scoop out the seeds. Set the zucchini in a greased baking pan, stuff each with the beef, scatter enchilada sauce on top, and spread with the Monterey cheese. 3. Bake in the oven at 350°F for 20 minutes while covered. Uncover, spread with cilantro, and bake for 5 minutes. Top with tomatoes, green onions and avocado, place on serving plates and enjoy.

Per Serving:

calories: 422 | fat: 33g | protein: 39g | carbs: 15g | net carbs: 8g | fiber: 7g

Mascarpone Pork Chops

Preparation time: 10 minutes | Cook time: 12 minutes | Serves 3

- ✓ 3 pork chops
- ✓ 1 tablespoon mascarpone cheese
- ✓ 1 teaspoon ground peppercorns
- ✓ ½ teaspoon dried sage
- ✓ 1 tablespoon olive oil

Instructions

1. In the shallow bowl, mix up peppercorns, dried sage, olive oil, and mascarpone cheese. 2. Brush the pork chops with the cheese mixture well and transfer in the instant pot. 3. Cook the meat on Sauté mode for 5 minutes from each side. 4. Then add the remaining cream cheese mixture and cook the pork chops for 2 minutes more.

Per Serving:

calories: 324 | fat: 18g | protein: 40g | carbs: 0g | net carbs: 0g | fiber: 0g

CHAPTER 4 Fish and Seafood

Crab-Stuffed Avocado Boats

Preparation time: 5 minutes | Cook time: 7 minutes | Serves 4

- ✓ 2 medium avocados, halved and pitted
- ✓ 8 ounces (227 g) cooked crab meat
- ✓ ¼ teaspoon Old Bay seasoning
- ✓ 2 tablespoons peeled and diced yellow onion
- ✓ 2 tablespoons mayonnaise

Instructions

1. Scoop out avocado flesh in each avocado half, leaving ½ inch around edges to form a shell. Chop scooped-out avocado. 2. In a medium bowl, combine crab meat, Old Bay seasoning, onion, mayonnaise, and chopped avocado. Place ¼ mixture into each avocado shell. 3. Place avocado boats into ungreased air fryer basket. Adjust the temperature to 350°F (177°C) and air fry for 7 minutes. Avocado will be browned on the top and mixture will be bubbling when done. Serve warm.

Per Serving:

calories: 272 | fat: 21g | protein: 11g | carbs: 9g | net carbs: 6g | fiber: 3g

Snapper in Spicy Tomato Sauce

Preparation time: 5 minutes | Cook time: 5 minutes | Serves 6

- ✓ 2 teaspoons coconut oil, melted
- ✓ 1 teaspoon celery seeds
- ✓ ½ teaspoon fresh grated ginger
- ✓ ½ teaspoon cumin seeds
- ✓ 1 yellow onion, chopped
- ✓ 2 cloves garlic, minced
- ✓ 1½ pounds (680 g) snapper fillets
- ✓ ¾ cup vegetable broth
- ✓ 1 (4-ounce / 113-g) can fire-roasted diced tomatoes
- ✓ 1 bell pepper, sliced
- ✓ 1 jalapeño pepper, minced

- ✓ Sea salt and ground black pepper, to taste
- ✓ ¼ teaspoon chili flakes
- ✓ ½ teaspoon turmeric powder

Instructions

1. Set the Instant Pot to Sauté. Add and heat the sesame oil until hot. Sauté the celery seeds, fresh ginger, and cumin seeds. 2. Add the onion and continue to sauté until softened and fragrant. 3. Mix in the minced garlic and continue to cook for 30 seconds. Add the remaining ingredients and stir well. 4. Lock the lid. Select the Manual mode and set the cooking time for 3 minutes at Low Pressure. 5. When the timer beeps, perform a quick pressure release. Carefully remove the lid. 6. Serve warm.

Per Serving:

calories: 177 | fat: 6g | protein: 26g | carbs: 5g | net carbs: 4g | fiber: 1g

Shrimp Stuffed Zucchini

Preparation time: 15 minutes | Cook time: 25 minutes | Serves 4

- ✓ 4 medium zucchinis
- ✓ 1 pound small shrimp, peeled, deveined
- ✓ 1 tablespoon minced onion
- ✓ 2 teaspoons butter
- ✓ ¼ cup chopped tomatoes
- ✓ Salt and black pepper to taste
- ✓ 1 cup pork rinds, crushed
- ✓ 1 tablespoon chopped basil leaves
- ✓ 2 tablespoons melted butter

Instructions

1. Preheat the oven to 350°F and trim off the top and bottom ends of the zucchinis. Lay them flat on a chopping board, and cut a ¼ -inch off the top to create a boat for the stuffing. Scoop out the seeds with a spoon and set the zucchinis aside. 2. Melt the firm butter in a small skillet and sauté the onion and tomato for 6 minutes. Transfer the mixture to a bowl and add the shrimp, half of the pork rinds, basil

leaves, salt, and black pepper. 3. Combine the ingredients and stuff the zucchini boats with the mixture. Sprinkle the top of the boats with the remaining pork rinds and drizzle the melted butter over them. 4. Place on a baking sheet and bake for 15 to 20 minutes. The shrimp should no longer be pink by this time. Remove the zucchinis after and serve with a tomato and mozzarella salad.

Per Serving:

calories: 300 | fat: 16g | protein: 26g | carbs: 10g | net carbs: 6g | fiber: 4g

Salmon Steaks with Garlicky Yogurt

Preparation time: 2 minutes | Cook time: 4 minutes | Serves 4

- ✓ 1 cup water
- ✓ 2 tablespoons olive oil
- ✓ 4 salmon steaks
- ✓ Coarse sea salt and ground black pepper, to taste
- ✓ Garlicky Yogurt:
- ✓ 1 (8-ounce / 227-g) container full-fat Greek yogurt
- ✓ 2 cloves garlic, minced
- ✓ 2 tablespoons mayonnaise
- ✓ ⅓ teaspoon Dijon mustard

Instructions

1. Pour the water into the Instant Pot and insert a trivet. 2. Rub the olive oil into the fish and sprinkle with the salt and black pepper on all sides. Put the fish on the trivet. 3. Lock the lid. Select the Manual mode and set the cooking time for 4 minutes at High Pressure. 4. When the timer beeps, perform a quick pressure release. Carefully remove the lid. 5. Meanwhile, stir together all the ingredients for the garlicky yogurt in a bowl. 6. Serve the salmon steaks alongside the garlicky yogurt.

Per Serving:

calories: 128 | fat: 11g | protein: 3g | carbs: 5g | net carbs: 5g | fiber: 0g

Snapper Scampi

Preparation time: 5 minutes | Cook time: 8 to

10 minutes | Serves 4

- ✓ 4 (6 ounces / 170 g) skinless snapper or arctic char fillets
- ✓ 1 tablespoon olive oil
- ✓ 3 tablespoons lemon juice, divided
- ✓ ½ teaspoon dried basil
- ✓ Pinch salt
- ✓ Freshly ground black pepper, to taste
- ✓ 2 tablespoons butter
- ✓ 2 cloves garlic, minced

Instructions

1. Rub the fish fillets with olive oil and 1 tablespoon of the lemon juice. Sprinkle with the basil, salt, and pepper, and place in the air fryer basket. 2. Air fry the fish at 380°F (193°C) for 7 to 8 minutes or until the fish just flakes when tested with a fork. Remove the fish from the basket and put on a serving plate. Cover to keep warm. 3. In a baking pan, combine the butter, remaining 2 tablespoons lemon juice, and garlic. Bake in the air fryer for 1 to 2 minutes or until the garlic is sizzling. Pour this mixture over the fish and serve

Per Serving:

calories: 256 | fat: 11g | protein: 35g | carbs: 1g | net carbs: 1g | fiber: 0g

Tuna Stuffed Poblano Peppers

Preparation time: 15 minutes | Cook time: 12 minutes | Serves 4

- ✓ 7 ounces (198 g) canned tuna, shredded
- ✓ 1 teaspoon cream cheese
- ✓ ¼ teaspoon minced garlic
- ✓ 2 ounces (57 g) Provolone cheese, grated
- ✓ 4 poblano pepper
- ✓ 1 cup water, for cooking

Instructions

1. Remove the seeds from poblano peppers. 2. In the mixing bowl, mix up shredded tuna, cream cheese, minced garlic, and grated cheese. 3. Then fill the peppers with tuna mixture and put it in the baking pan. 4. Pour water and insert the baking pan in the instant pot. 5. Cook the meal on Manual mode (High Pressure) for 12 minutes. Then make a quick

pressure release.

Per Serving:

calories: 153 | fat: 8g | protein: 17g | carbs: 2g | net carbs: 1g | fiber: 1g

Pecan-Crusted Catfish

Preparation time: 5 minutes | Cook time: 12 minutes | Serves 4

- ✓ ½ cup pecan meal
- ✓ 1 teaspoon fine sea salt
- ✓ ¼ teaspoon ground black pepper
- ✓ 4 (4 ounces / 113 g) catfish fillets
- ✓ For Garnish (Optional):
- ✓ Fresh oregano
- ✓ Pecan halves

Instructions

1. Spray the air fryer basket with avocado oil. Preheat the air fryer to 375°F (191°C). 2. In a large bowl, mix the pecan meal, salt, and pepper. One at a time, dredge the catfish fillets in the mixture, coating them well. Use your hands to press the pecan meal into the fillets. Spray the fish with avocado oil and place them in the air fryer basket. 3. Air fry the coated catfish for 12 minutes, or until it flakes easily and is no longer translucent in the center, flipping halfway through. 4. Garnish with oregano sprigs and pecan halves, if desired. 5. Store leftovers in an airtight container in the fridge for up to 3 days. Reheat in a preheated 350°F (177°C) air fryer for 4 minutes, or until heated through.

Per Serving:

calories: 390 | fat: 28g | protein: 27g | carbs: 6g | net carbs: 4g | fiber: 2g

Salmon Fillets and Bok Choy

Preparation time: 5 minutes | Cook time: 8 minutes | Serves 4

- ✓ 1½ cups water
- ✓ 2 tablespoons unsalted butter
- ✓ 4 (1-inch thick) salmon fillets
- ✓ ½ teaspoon cayenne pepper
- ✓ Sea salt and freshly ground pepper, to taste
- ✓ 2 cups Bok choy, sliced

- ✓ 1 cup chicken broth
- ✓ 3 cloves garlic, minced
- ✓ 1 teaspoon grated lemon zest
- ✓ ½ teaspoon dried dill weed

Instructions

1. Pour the water into your Instant Pot and insert a trivet. 2. Brush the salmon with the melted butter and season with the cayenne pepper, salt, and black pepper on all sides. 3. Lock the lid. Select the Manual mode and set the cooking time for 3 minutes at Low Pressure. 4. When the timer beeps, perform a quick pressure release. Carefully remove the lid. 5. Add the remaining ingredients. 6. Lock the lid. Select the Manual mode and set the cooking time for 5 minutes at High Pressure. 7. When the timer beeps, perform a quick pressure release. Carefully remove the lid. 8. Serve the poached salmon with the veggies on the side.

Per Serving:

calories: 209 | fat: 11g | protein: 24g | carbs: 2g | net carbs: 2g | fiber: 1g

Parmesan-Crusted Salmon

Preparation time: 5 minutes | Cook time: 20 minutes | Serves 2

- ✓ 2 tablespoons mayonnaise
- ✓ 1 tablespoon grated Parmesan cheese
- ✓ 1 tablespoon shredded Parmesan cheese
- ✓ 1 teaspoon freshly squeezed lemon juice
- ✓ ½ teaspoon dried parsley
- ✓ ½ teaspoon minced garlic
- ✓ Pink Himalayan sea salt
- ✓ Freshly ground black pepper
- ✓ 2 (8-ounce / 227-g) salmon fillets, skin on

Instructions

1. Preheat the oven to 400°F (205°C). Line a baking sheet with aluminum foil. 2. In a small bowl, combine the mayonnaise, both types of Parmesan, lemon juice, parsley, and garlic. Season with salt and pepper. 3. Place the salmon skin-side down on the baking sheet. Spread the sauce evenly across both fillets. 4. Bake for 15 to 17 minutes, until the salmon flakes easily with a fork. Serve immediately.

Per Serving:

calories: 584 | fat: 40g | protein: 53g | carbs: 1g | net carbs: 1g | fiber: 0g

Tandoori Shrimp

Preparation time: 25 minutes | Cook time: 6 minutes | Serves 4

✓ 1 pound (454 g) jumbo raw shrimp (21 to 25 count), peeled and deveined

✓ 1 tablespoon minced fresh ginger

✓ 3 cloves garlic, minced

✓ ¼ cup chopped fresh cilantro or parsley, plus more for garnish

✓ 1 teaspoon ground turmeric

✓ 1 teaspoon garam masala

✓ 1 teaspoon smoked paprika

✓ 1 teaspoon kosher salt

✓ ½ to 1 teaspoon cayenne pepper

✓ 2 tablespoons olive oil (for Paleo) or melted ghee

✓ 2 teaspoons fresh lemon juice

Instructions

1. In a large bowl, combine the shrimp, ginger, garlic, cilantro, turmeric, garam masala, paprika, salt, and cayenne. Toss well to coat. Add the oil or ghee and toss again. Marinate at room temperature for 15 minutes, or cover and refrigerate for up to 8 hours. 2. Place the shrimp in a single layer in the air fryer basket. Set the air fryer to 325°F (163°C) for 6 minutes. Transfer the shrimp to a serving platter. Cover and let the shrimp finish cooking in the residual heat, about 5 minutes. 3. Sprinkle the shrimp with the lemon juice and toss to coat. Garnish with additional cilantro and serve.

Per Serving:

calories: 167 | fat: 7g | protein: 23g | carbs: 2g | net carbs: 1g | fiber: 1g

Cod Fillet with Olives

Preparation time: 15 minutes | Cook time: 10 minutes | Serves 2

✓ 8 ounces (227 g) cod fillet

✓ ¼ cup sliced olives

✓ 1 teaspoon olive oil

✓ ¼ teaspoon salt

✓ 1 cup water, for cooking

Instructions

1. Pour water and insert the steamer rack in the instant pot. 2. Then cut the cod fillet into 2 servings and sprinkle with salt and olive oil. 3. Then place the fish on the foil and top with the sliced olives. Wrap the fish and transfer it in the steamer rack. 4. Close and seal the lid. Cook the fish on Manual mode (High Pressure) for 10 minutes. 5. Allow the natural pressure release for 5 minutes.

Per Serving:

calories: 130 | fat: 5g | protein: 20g | carbs: 1g | net carbs: 1g | fiber: 0g

Coconut Crab Patties

Preparation time: 5 minutes | Cook time: 6 minutes | Serves 8

✓ 2 tablespoons coconut oil

✓ 1 tablespoon lemon juice

✓ 1cup lump crab meat

✓ 2 teaspoons Dijon mustard

✓ 1 egg, beaten

✓ 1½ tablespoons coconut flour

Instructions

1. In a bowl to the crabmeat, add all the ingredients, except for the oil; mix well to combine. Make patties out of the mixture. Melt the coconut oil in a skillet over medium heat. Add the crab patties and cook for about 2-3 minutes per side.

Per Serving:

calories: 209 | fat: 13g | protein: 17g | carbs: 6g | net carbs: 4g | fiber: 2g

Roasted Salmon with Avocado Salsa

Preparation time: 10 minutes | Cook time: 12 minutes | Serves 4

✓ For The Salsa

✓ 1 avocado, peeled, pitted, and diced

✓ 1 scallion, white and green parts, chopped

✓ ½ cup halved cherry tomatoes

✓ Juice of 1 lemon

- ✓ Zest of 1 lemon
- ✓ For The Fish
- ✓ 1 teaspoon ground cumin
- ✓ ½ teaspoon ground coriander
- ✓ ½ teaspoon onion powder
- ✓ ¼ teaspoon sea salt
- ✓ Pinch freshly ground black pepper
- ✓ Pinch cayenne pepper
- ✓ 4 (4-ounce) boneless, skinless salmon fillets
- ✓ 2 tablespoons olive oil

Make The Salsa: Instructions

1. In a small bowl, stir together the avocado, scallion, tomatoes, lemon juice, and lemon zest until mixed. 2. Set aside. Make The Fish: Instructions

1. Preheat the oven to 400°F. Line a baking sheet with aluminum foil and set aside. 2. In a small bowl, stir together the cumin, coriander, onion powder, salt, black pepper, and cayenne until well mixed. 3. Rub the salmon fillets with the spice mix and place them on the baking sheet. 4. Drizzle the fillets with the olive oil and roast the fish until it is just cooked through, about 15 minutes. 5. Serve the salmon topped with the avocado salsa.

Per Serving:

calories: 320 | fat: 26g | protein: 22g | carbs: 4g | net carbs: 1g | fiber: 3g

Coconut Curry Mussels

Preparation time: 15 minutes | Cook time: 12 minutes | Serves 6

- ✓ 3 pounds mussels, cleaned, de-bearded
- ✓ 1 cup minced shallots
- ✓ 3 tablespoons minced garlic
- ✓ 1½ cups coconut milk
- ✓ 2 cups dry white wine
- ✓ 2 teaspoons red curry powder
- ✓ ⅓ cup coconut oil
- ✓ ⅓ cup chopped green onions
- ✓ ⅓ cup chopped parsley

Instructions

1. Pour the wine into a large saucepan and cook the shallots and garlic over low heat. Stir in the coconut milk and red curry powder and cook for 3 minutes. 2.

Add the mussels and steam for 7 minutes or until their shells are opened. Then, use a slotted spoon to remove to a bowl leaving the sauce in the pan. Discard any closed mussels at this point. 3. Stir the coconut oil into the sauce, turn the heat off, and stir in the parsley and green onions. Serve the sauce immediately with a butternut squash mash.

Per Serving:

calories: 275 | fat: 19g | protein: 23g | carbs: 3g | net carbs: 2g | fiber: 1g

Chili and Turmeric Haddock

Preparation time: 10 minutes | Cook time: 5 minutes | Serves 4

- ✓ 1 chili pepper, minced
- ✓ 1 pound (454 g) haddock, chopped
- ✓ ½ teaspoon ground turmeric
- ✓ ⅓ cup fish stock
- ✓ 1 cup water

Instructions

1. In the mixing bowl mix up chili pepper, ground turmeric, and fish stock. 2. Then add chopped haddock and transfer the mixture in the baking mold. 3. Pour water in the instant pot and insert the trivet. 4. Place the baking mold with fish on the trivet and close the lid. 5. Cook the meal on Manual (High Pressure) for 5 minutes. Make a quick pressure release.

Per Serving:

calories: 130 | fat: 1g | protein: 28g | carbs: 0g | net carbs: 0g | fiber: 0g

South Indian Fried Fish

Preparation time: 20 minutes | Cook time: 8 minutes | Serves 4

- ✓ 2 tablespoons olive oil
- ✓ 2 tablespoons fresh lime or lemon juice
- ✓ 1 teaspoon minced fresh ginger
- ✓ 1 clove garlic, minced
- ✓ 1 teaspoon ground turmeric
- ✓ ½ teaspoon kosher salt
- ✓ ¼ to ½ teaspoon cayenne pepper
- ✓ 1 pound (454 g) tilapia fillets (2 to 3 fillets)

✓ Olive oil spray

✓ Lime or lemon wedges (optional)

Instructions

1. In a large bowl, combine the oil, lime juice, ginger, garlic, turmeric, salt, and cayenne. Stir until well combined; set aside. 2. Cut each tilapia fillet into three or four equal-size pieces. Add the fish to the bowl and gently mix until all of the fish is coated in the marinade. Marinate for 10 to 15 minutes at room temperature. (Don't marinate any longer or the acid in the lime juice will "cook" the fish.) 3. Spray the air fryer basket with olive oil spray. Place the fish in the basket and spray the fish. Set the air fryer to 325°F (163°C) for 3 minutes to partially cook the fish. Set the air fryer to 400°F (204°C) for 5 minutes to finish cooking and crisp up the fish. (Thinner pieces of fish will cook faster so you may want to check at the 3-minute mark of the second cooking time and remove those that are cooked through, and then add them back toward the end of the second cooking time to crisp.) 4. Carefully remove the fish from the basket. Serve hot, with lemon wedges if desired.

Per Serving:

calories: 161 | fat: 8g | protein: 22g | carbs: 2g | net carbs: 1g | fiber: 1g

Cajun Salmon

Preparation time: 5 minutes | Cook time: 7 minutes | Serves 2

✓ 2 (4 ounces / 113 g) salmon fillets, skin removed

✓ 2 tablespoons unsalted butter, melted

✓ ⅛ teaspoon ground cayenne pepper

✓ ½ teaspoon garlic powder

✓ 1 teaspoon paprika

✓ ¼ teaspoon ground black pepper

Instructions

1. Brush each fillet with butter. 2. Combine remaining ingredients in a small bowl and then rub onto fish. Place fillets into the air fryer basket. 3. Adjust the temperature to 390°F (199°C) and air fry for 7 minutes. 4. When fully cooked, internal temperature will be 145°F (63°C). Serve

immediately.

Per Serving:

calories: 213 | fat: 12g | protein: 24g | carbs: 1g | net carbs: 0g | fiber: 1g

Salmon Oscar

Preparation time: 5 minutes | Cook time: 20 minutes | Serves 2

✓ ¼ cup (½ stick) butter

✓ 1 tablespoon finely minced onion

✓ 1½ teaspoons white wine vinegar

✓ 1 teaspoon freshly squeezed lemon juice

✓ ½ teaspoon dried tarragon

✓ ¼ teaspoon dried parsley

✓ 1 large egg yolk

✓ 2 tablespoons heavy (whipping) cream

✓ 1 tablespoon extra-virgin olive oil

✓ 2 (8-ounce / 227-g) salmon fillets

✓ Pink Himalayan sea salt

✓ Freshly ground black pepper

✓ 1 (6- to 8-ounce / 170- to 227-g) container lump crab meat

Instructions

1. In a small saucepan, melt the butter over medium heat. 2. Add the onion and cook for 3 to 5 minutes, until it begins to turn translucent. Add the vinegar, lemon juice, tarragon, and parsley. Stir to combine. 3. In a small bowl, whisk together the egg yolk and cream. 4. Once the mixture in the saucepan starts to simmer, remove it from the heat and slowly add the egg mixture, whisking while you pour. Continue to whisk for 2 to 3 minutes, until the sauce thickens. Cover and set aside. 5. Season the salmon fillets with salt and pepper. 6. In a medium sauté pan or skillet, heat the olive oil over medium-high heat. Place the fillets skin-side up in the skillet. Cook for 4 to 5 minutes, then turn and cook for an additional 4 to 5 minutes on the other side, until the flesh flakes easily with a fork. 7. Transfer the salmon to a serving plate, then place the crab in the skillet and quickly heat it, stirring gently. 8. Top the salmon fillets with the crab, then drizzle on the sauce. Serve at once.

Per Serving:

calories: 741 | fat: 53g | protein: 62g | carbs: 1g | net carbs: 1g | fiber: 0g

Halibut Curry

Preparation time: 5 minutes | Cook time: 35 minutes | Serves 4

- ✓ 1 tablespoon avocado oil
- ✓ ½ cup finely chopped celery
- ✓ ½ cup frozen butternut squash cubes
- ✓ 1 cup full-fat coconut milk
- ✓ ½ cup seafood stock
- ✓ 1½ tablespoons curry powder
- ✓ 1 tablespoon dried cilantro
- ✓ ½ tablespoon garlic powder
- ✓ ½ tablespoon ground turmeric
- ✓ 1 teaspoon ground ginger
- ✓ 1 pound (454 g) skinless halibut fillet, cut into chunks
- ✓ Cooked cauliflower rice, for serving (optional)

Instructions

1. In a large pot with a lid, heat the avocado oil over medium-high heat. Add the celery and cook for about 3 minutes. Add the squash and cook for 5 minutes more. 2. Pour in the coconut milk and seafood stock and cook, stirring, for another 3 minutes. Stir in the curry powder, cilantro, garlic, turmeric, and ginger. 3. Add the halibut to the pot and stir into the rest of the mixture. Reduce the heat to medium, cover the pot, and cook for 15 to 20 minutes, or until the fish is completely white and flakes easily with a fork. 4. Serve the halibut curry over cauliflower rice if you'd like, or just eat it by itself!

Per Serving:

calories: 362 | fat: 22g | protein: 33g | carbs: 8g | net carbs: 5g | fiber: 3g

Rainbow Salmon Kebabs

Preparation time: 10 minutes | Cook time: 8 minutes | Serves 2

- ✓ 6 ounces (170 g) boneless, skinless salmon, cut into 1-inch cubes
- ✓ ¼ medium red onion, peeled and cut into 1-inch pieces
- ✓ ½ medium yellow bell pepper, seeded and cut into 1-inch pieces
- ✓ ½ medium zucchini, trimmed and cut into ½-inch slices
- ✓ 1 tablespoon olive oil
- ✓ ½ teaspoon salt
- ✓ ¼ teaspoon ground black pepper

Instructions

1. Using one (6-inch) skewer, skewer 1 piece salmon, then 1 piece onion, 1 piece bell pepper, and finally 1 piece zucchini. Repeat this pattern with additional skewers to make four kebabs total. Drizzle with olive oil and sprinkle with salt and black pepper. 2. Place kebabs into ungreased air fryer basket. Adjust the temperature to 400°F (204°C) and air fry for 8 minutes, turning kebabs halfway through cooking. Salmon will easily flake and have an internal temperature of at least 145°F (63°C) when done; vegetables will be tender. Serve warm.

Per Serving:

calories: 270 | fat: 16g | protein: 25g | carbs: 9g | net carbs: 6g | fiber: 3g

Cod with Parsley Pistou

Preparation time: 15 minutes | Cook time: 10 minutes | Serves 4

- ✓ 1 cup packed roughly chopped fresh flat-leaf Italian parsley
- ✓ 1 to 2 small garlic cloves, minced
- ✓ Zest and juice of 1 lemon
- ✓ 1 teaspoon salt
- ✓ ½ teaspoon freshly ground black pepper
- ✓ 1 cup extra-virgin olive oil, divided
- ✓ 1 pound (454 g) cod fillets, cut into 4 equal-sized pieces

Instructions

1. In a food processer, combine the parsley, garlic, lemon zest and juice, salt, and pepper. Pulse to chop well. 2. While the food processor is running, slowly stream in ¾ cup olive oil until well combined. Set aside. 3. In a large skillet, heat the remaining ¼ cup olive oil over medium-high heat. Add the cod fillets,

cover, and cook 4 to 5 minutes on each side, or until cooked through. Thicker fillets may require a bit more cooking time. Remove from the heat and keep warm. 4. Add the pistou to the skillet and heat over medium-low heat. Return the cooked fish to the skillet, flipping to coat in the sauce. Serve warm, covered with pistou.

Per Serving:

calories: 550 | fat: 50g | protein: 21g | carbs: 4g | net carbs: 3g | fiber: 1g

Cod with Jalapeño

Preparation time: 5 minutes | Cook time: 14 minutes | Serves 4

✓ 4 cod fillets, boneless
✓ 1 jalapeño, minced
✓ 1 tablespoon avocado oil
✓ ½ teaspoon minced garlic

Instructions

1. In the shallow bowl, mix minced jalapeño, avocado oil, and minced garlic. 2. Put the cod fillets in the air fryer basket in one layer and top with minced jalapeño mixture. 3. Cook the fish at 365°F (185°C) for 7 minutes per side.

Per Serving:

calories: 130 | fat: 3g | protein: 23g | carbs: 0g | net carbs: 0g | fiber: 0g

Dill Salmon Cakes

Preparation time: 15 minutes | Cook time: 10 minutes | Serves 4

✓ 1 pound (454 g) salmon fillet, chopped
✓ 1 tablespoon chopped dill
✓ 2 eggs, beaten
✓ ½ cup almond flour
✓ 1 tablespoon coconut oil

Instructions

1. Put the chopped salmon, dill, eggs, and almond flour in the food processor. 2. Blend the mixture until it is smooth. 3. Then make the small balls (cakes) from the salmon mixture. 4. After this, heat up the coconut oil on Sauté mode for 3 minutes. 5. Put the salmon cakes in the instant pot in one layer

and cook them on Sauté mode for 2 minutes from each side or until they are light brown.

Per Serving:

calories: 297 | fat: 19g | protein: 28g | carbs: 4g | net carbs: 2g | fiber: 2g

Aromatic Monkfish Stew

Preparation time: 5 minutes | Cook time: 6 minutes | Serves 6

✓ Juice of 1 lemon
✓ 1 tablespoon fresh basil
✓ 1 tablespoon fresh parsley
✓ 1 tablespoon olive oil
✓ 1 teaspoon garlic, minced
✓ 1½ pounds (680 g) monkfish
✓ 1 tablespoon butter
✓ 1 bell pepper, chopped
✓ 1 onion, sliced
✓ ½ teaspoon cayenne pepper
✓ ½ teaspoon mixed peppercorns
✓ ¼ teaspoon turmeric powder
✓ ¼ teaspoon ground cumin
✓ Sea salt and ground black pepper, to taste
✓ 2 cups fish stock
✓ ½ cup water
✓ ¼ cup dry white wine
✓ 2 bay leaves
✓ 1 ripe tomato, crushed

Instructions

1. Stir together the lemon juice, basil, parsley, olive oil, and garlic in a ceramic dish. Add the monkfish and marinate for 30 minutes. 2. Set your Instant Pot to Sauté. Add and melt the butter. Once hot, cook the bell pepper and onion until fragrant. 3. Stir in the remaining ingredients. 4. Lock the lid. Select the Manual mode and set the cooking time for 6 minutes at High Pressure. 5. When the timer beeps, perform a quick pressure release. Carefully remove the lid. 6. Discard the bay leaves and divide your stew into serving bowls. Serve hot.

Per Serving:

calories: 153 | fat: 7g | protein: 19g | carbs: 4g | net carbs: 3g | fiber: 1g

Sardine Fritter Wraps

Preparation time: 5 minutes | Cook time: 8 minutes | Serves 4

- ✓ ⅓ cup (80 ml) refined avocado oil, for frying
- ✓ Fritters:
- ✓ 2 (4.375 ounces/125 g) cans sardines, drained
- ✓ ½ cup (55 g) blanched almond flour
- ✓ 2 large eggs
- ✓ 2 tablespoons finely chopped fresh parsley
- ✓ 2 tablespoons finely diced red bell pepper
- ✓ 2 cloves garlic, minced
- ✓ ½ teaspoon finely ground gray sea salt
- ✓ ¼ teaspoon ground black pepper
- ✓ For Serving:
- ✓ 8 romaine lettuce leaves
- ✓ 1 small English cucumber, sliced thin
- ✓ 8 tablespoons (105 g) mayonnaise
- ✓ Thinly sliced green onions

Instructions

1. Pour the avocado oil into a large frying pan. Heat on medium for a couple of minutes. 2. Meanwhile, prepare the fritters: Place the fritter ingredients in a medium-sized bowl and stir to combine, being careful not to mash the heck out of the sardines. Spoon about 1 tablespoon of the mixture into the palm of your hand and roll it into a ball, then flatten it like a burger patty. Repeat with the remaining fritter mixture, making a total of 16 small patties. 3. Fry the fritters in the hot oil for 2 minutes per side, then transfer to a cooling rack. You may have to fry the fritters in batches if your pan isn't large enough to fit them all without overcrowding. 4. Meanwhile, divide the lettuce leaves among 4 dinner plates. Top with the sliced cucumber. When the fritters are done, place 2 fritters on each leaf. Top with a dollop of mayonnaise, sprinkle with sliced green onions, and serve!

Per Serving:

calories: 612 | fat: 56g | protein: 23g | carbs: 6g | net carbs: 4g | fiber: 2g

Ginger Cod

Preparation time: 10 minutes | Cook time: 20 minutes | Serves 2

- ✓ 1 teaspoon ginger paste
- ✓ 8 ounces (227 g) cod fillet, chopped
- ✓ 1 tablespoon coconut oil
- ✓ ¼ cup coconut milk

Instructions

1. Melt the coconut oil in the instant pot on Sauté mode. 2. Then add ginger paste and coconut milk and bring the mixture to boil. 3. Add chopped cod and sauté the meal for 12 minutes. Stir the fish cubes with the help of the spatula from time to time.

Per Serving:

calories: 222 | fat: 15g | protein: 21g | carbs: 2g | net carbs: 1g | fiber: 1g

Coconut Shrimp Curry

Preparation time: 10 minutes | Cook time: 4 minutes | Serves 5

- ✓ 15 ounces (425 g) shrimp, peeled
- ✓ 1 teaspoon chili powder
- ✓ 1 teaspoon garam masala
- ✓ 1 cup coconut milk
- ✓ 1 teaspoon olive oil
- ✓ ½ teaspoon minced garlic

Instructions

1. Heat up the instant pot on Sauté mode for 2 minutes. 2. Then add olive oil. Cook the ingredients for 1 minute. 3. Add shrimp and sprinkle them with chili powder, garam masala, minced garlic, and coconut milk. 4. Carefully stir the ingredients and close the lid. 5. Cook the shrimp curry on Manual mode for 1 minute. Make a quick pressure release.

Per Serving:

calories: 222 | fat: 14g | protein: 21g | carbs: 4g | net carbs: 3g | fiber: 1g

Shrimp Ceviche Salad

Preparation time: 15 minutes | Cook time: 0 minutes | Serves 4

- ✓ 1 pound (454 g) fresh shrimp, peeled and deveined

- ✓ 1 small red or yellow bell pepper, cut into ½-inch chunks
- ✓ ½ English cucumber, peeled and cut into ½-inch chunks
- ✓ ½ small red onion, cut into thin slivers
- ✓ ¼ cup chopped fresh cilantro or flat-leaf Italian parsley
- ✓ ⅓ cup freshly squeezed lime juice
- ✓ 2 tablespoons freshly squeezed lemon juice
- ✓ 2 tablespoons freshly squeezed clementine juice or orange juice
- ✓ ½ cup extra-virgin olive oil
- ✓ 1 teaspoon salt
- ✓ ½ teaspoon freshly ground black pepper
- ✓ 2 ripe avocados, peeled, pitted, and cut into ½-inch chunks

Instructions

1. Cut the shrimp in half lengthwise. In a large glass bowl, combine the shrimp, bell pepper, cucumber, onion, and cilantro. 2. In a small bowl, whisk together the lime, lemon, and clementine juices, olive oil, salt, and pepper. Pour the mixture over the shrimp and veggies and toss to coat. Cover and refrigerate for at least 2 hours, or up to 8 hours. Give the mixture a toss every 30 minutes for the first 2 hours to make sure all the shrimp "cook" in the juices. 3. Add the cut avocado just before serving and toss to combine.

Per Serving:

calories: 490 | fat: 36g | protein: 28g | carbs: 17g | net carbs: 11g | fiber: 6g

Grilled Calamari

Preparation time: 10 minutes | Cook time: 5 minutes | Serves 4

- ✓ 2 pounds calamari tubes and tentacles, cleaned
- ✓ ½ cup good-quality olive oil
- ✓ Zest and juice of 2 lemons
- ✓ 2 tablespoons chopped fresh oregano
- ✓ 1 tablespoon minced garlic
- ✓ ¼ teaspoon sea salt
- ✓ ⅛ teaspoon freshly ground black pepper

Instructions

1. Prepare the calamari. Score the top layer of the calamari tubes about 2 inches apart. 2. Marinate the calamari. In a large bowl, stir together the olive oil, lemon zest, lemon juice, oregano, garlic, salt, and pepper. Add the calamari and toss to coat it well, then place it in the refrigerator to marinate for at least 30 minutes and up to 1 hour. 3. Grill the calamari. Preheat a grill to high heat. Grill the calamari, turning once, for about 3 minutes total, until it's tender and lightly charred. 4. Serve. Divide the calamari between four plates and serve it hot.

Per Serving:

calories: 455 | fat: 30g | protein: 35g | carbs: 8g | net carbs: 7g | fiber: 1g

Blackened Salmon

Preparation time: 10 minutes | Cook time: 8 minutes | Serves 2

- ✓ 10 ounces (283 g) salmon fillet
- ✓ ½ teaspoon ground coriander
- ✓ 1 teaspoon ground cumin
- ✓ 1 teaspoon dried basil
- ✓ 1 tablespoon avocado oil

Instructions

1. In the shallow bowl, mix ground coriander, ground cumin, and dried basil. 2. Then coat the salmon fillet in the spices and sprinkle with avocado oil. 3. Put the fish in the air fryer basket and cook at 395°F (202°C) for 4 minutes per side.

Per Serving:

calories: 270 | fat: 17g | protein: 25g | carbs: 2g | net carbs: 0g | fiber: 2g

CHAPTER 5 Snacks and Appetizers

Roasted Garlic Bulbs

Preparation time: 2 minutes | Cook time: 25 minutes | Serves 4

- ✓ 4 bulbs garlic
- ✓ 1 tablespoon avocado oil
- ✓ 1 teaspoon salt
- ✓ Pinch of black pepper
- ✓ 1 cup water

Instructions

1. Slice the pointy tops off the bulbs of garlic to expose the cloves. 2. Drizzle the avocado oil on top of the garlic and sprinkle with the salt and pepper. 3. Place the bulbs in the steamer basket, cut side up. Alternatively, you may place them on a piece of aluminum foil with the sides pulled up and resting on top of the trivet. Place the steamer basket in the pot. 4. Close the lid and seal the vent. Cook on High Pressure for 25 minutes. Quick release the steam. 5. Let the garlic cool completely before removing the bulbs from the pot. 6. Hold the stem end (bottom) of the bulb and squeeze out all the garlic. Mash the cloves with a fork to make a paste.

Per Serving:

calories: 44 | fat: 5g | protein: 0g | carbs: 1g | net carbs: 1g | fiber: 0g

Pizza Bites

Preparation time: 5 minutes | Cook time: 10 minutes | Makes 12 pizza bites

- ✓ 12 large pepperoni slices
- ✓ 2 tablespoons tomato paste
- ✓ 12 mini Mozzarella balls (approximately 8 ounces / 227 g)
- ✓ 12 fresh basil leaves (optional)

Instructions

1. Preheat the oven to 400°F (205°C). 2. Line each of 12 cups of a mini muffin pan with one pepperoni slice. To make them sit better, use kitchen shears to make three or four small cuts toward the center of the slice, but do not cut too far in—leave the center intact. 3. Bake 5 minutes, remove from the oven, and allow to cool in the pan for 5 to 10 minutes, until somewhat crisp. Keep the oven turned on. 4. Spoon ½ teaspoon of tomato paste into each pepperoni cup and gently spread to coat the bottom. Place a Mozzarella ball and a basil leaf, if using, in each cup. Return muffin pan to the oven and cook another 3 to 5 minutes, until the cheese is melting. 5. Remove pan from the oven and allow the bites to cool for 5 to 10 minutes before serving.

Per Serving:

calories: 198 | fat: 15g | protein: 11g | carbs: 0g | net carbs: 2g | fiber: 0g

Bacon Ranch Dip

Preparation time: 10 minutes | Cook time: 10 minutes | Serves 10

- ✓ 1 (8-ounce / 227-g) package full-fat cream cheese, at room temperature
- ✓ 1 cup full-fat sour cream
- ✓ 8 bacon slices, cooked and crumbled
- ✓ 1½ teaspoons dried chives
- ✓ 1 teaspoon dry mustard
- ✓ ½ teaspoon dried dill
- ✓ ½ teaspoon celery seed
- ✓ ½ teaspoon garlic powder
- ✓ ½ teaspoon onion powder
- ✓ Salt and freshly ground black pepper, to taste
- ✓ ¼ cup sliced scallion, or fresh chives, for garnish

Instructions

1. In a medium bowl, stir the cream cheese until it becomes fluffy and smooth. Add the sour cream and gently fold to combine. 2. Add the bacon, chives, mustard, dill, celery seed, garlic powder, and onion powder. Season with salt and pepper and stir to combine. Top with the scallion and serve

immediately, or refrigerate in an airtight container for up to 1 week.

Per Serving:

calories: 211 | fat: 19g | protein: 8g | carbs: 2g | net carbs: 2g | fiber: 0g

Cauliflower Cheese Balls

Preparation time: 5 minutes | Cook time: 21 minutes | Serves 8

- ✓ 1 cup water
- ✓ 1 head cauliflower, broken into florets
- ✓ 1 cup shredded Asiago cheese
- ✓ ½ cup grated Parmesan cheese
- ✓ 2 eggs, beaten
- ✓ 2 tablespoons butter
- ✓ 2 tablespoons minced fresh chives
- ✓ 1 garlic clove, minced
- ✓ ½ teaspoon cayenne pepper
- ✓ Coarse sea salt and white pepper, to taste

Instructions

1. Pour the water into the Instant Pot and insert a steamer basket. Place the cauliflower in the basket. 2. Lock the lid. Select the Manual mode and set the cooking time for 3 minutes at High Pressure. 3. When the timer beeps, perform a quick pressure release. Carefully remove the lid. 4. Transfer the cauliflower to a food processor, along with the remaining ingredients. Pulse until everything is well combined. 5. Form the mixture into bite-sized balls and place them on a baking sheet. 6. Bake in the preheated oven at 400°F (205°C) for 18 minutes until golden brown. Flip the balls halfway through the cooking time. Cool for 5 minutes before serving.

Per Serving:

calories: 161 | fat: 13g | protein: 9g | carbs: 4g | net carbs: 3g | fiber: 1g

Salami Chips with Pesto

Preparation time: 10 minutes | Cook time: 12 minutes | Serves 6

- ✓ Chips:
- ✓ 6 ounces sliced Genoa salami
- ✓ Pesto:

- ✓ 1 cup fresh basil leaves
- ✓ 3 cloves garlic
- ✓ ¼ cup grated Parmesan cheese
- ✓ ¼ cup raw walnuts
- ✓ ¼ teaspoon pink Himalayan salt
- ✓ ¼ teaspoon ground black pepper
- ✓ ½ cup extra-virgin olive oil

Instructions

1. Make the chips: Preheat the oven to 375°F and line 2 rimmed baking sheets with parchment paper. 2. Arrange the salami in a single layer on the lined baking sheets. Bake for 10 to 12 minutes, until crisp. Transfer to a paper towel–lined plate to absorb the excess oil. Allow to cool and crisp up further. 3. Make the pesto: Put all the pesto ingredients, except for the olive oil, in a food processor and pulse until everything is roughly chopped and a coarse paste has formed. 4. With the food processor running, slowly pour in the olive oil. Process until all of the oil has been added and the ingredients are fully incorporated. Taste and season with additional salt and pepper, if desired. 5. Pour the pesto into a small serving bowl and serve the salami chips alongside. Store leftover pesto in a sealed container in the refrigerator for up to 2 weeks; store the chips in a zip-top plastic bag in the refrigerator for up to 5 days.

Per Serving:

calories: 202 | fat: 9g | protein: 8g | carbs: 1g | net carbs: 1g | fiber: 0g

Hushpuppies

Preparation time: 10 minutes | Cook time: 15 minutes | Makes 10 hushpuppies

- ✓ High-quality oil, for frying
- ✓ 1 cup finely ground blanched almond flour
- ✓ 1 tablespoon coconut flour
- ✓ 1 teaspoon baking powder
- ✓ ½ teaspoon salt
- ✓ ¼ cup finely chopped onions
- ✓ ¼ cup heavy whipping cream
- ✓ 1 large egg, beaten

Instructions

1. Attach a candy thermometer to a Dutch oven or other large heavy pot, then pour in 3 inches of oil and set over medium-high heat. Heat the oil to 375°F. 2. In a medium-sized bowl, stir together the almond flour, coconut flour, baking powder, and salt. Stir in the rest of the ingredients and mix until blended. Do not overmix. 3. Use a tablespoon-sized cookie scoop to gently drop the batter into the hot oil. Don't overcrowd the hushpuppies; cook them in two batches. Fry for 3 minutes, then use a mesh skimmer or slotted spoon to turn and fry them for 3 more minutes or until golden brown on all sides. 4. Use the skimmer or slotted spoon to remove the hushpuppies from the oil and place on a paper towel–lined plate to drain. They are best served immediately.

Per Serving:

calories: 172 | fat: 12g | protein: 6g | carbs: 4g | net carbs: 3g | fiber: 3g

Devilish Eggs

Preparation time: 10 minutes | Cook time: 9 minutes | Serves 6

- ✓ 6 large eggs
- ✓ 3 tablespoons full-fat mayonnaise
- ✓ 1 teaspoon plain white vinegar
- ✓ 1 teaspoon spicy mustard
- ✓ ⅛ teaspoon salt
- ✓ ⅛ teaspoon black pepper
- ✓ ⅛ teaspoon ground cayenne
- ✓ ⅛ teaspoon paprika

Instructions

1. Preferred Method: Hard-boil eggs using a steamer basket in the Instant Pot® on high pressure for 9 minutes. Release pressure and remove eggs. 2. Alternate Method: Place eggs in a large pot. Cover with water by 1". Cover with a lid and place the pot over high heat until it reaches a boil. Turn off heat, leave covered, and let it sit for 13 minutes. Then, remove the eggs from the pan, place them in an ice water bath, and let them cool 5 minutes. 3. When cooled, peel eggs and slice in half lengthwise. Place yolks in a medium bowl. 4. Mash and mix yolks with

mayonnaise, vinegar, mustard, salt, and black pepper. 5. Scrape mixture into a sandwich-sized plastic bag and snip off one corner, making a hole about the width of a pencil. Use makeshift pastry bag to fill egg white halves with yolk mixture. 6. Garnish Devilish Eggs with cayenne and paprika (mostly for color) and serve.

Per Serving:

calories: 125| fat: 9g | protein: 6g | carbs: 1g | net carbs: 1g | fiber: 0g

Rosemary Chicken Wings

Preparation time: 10 minutes | Cook time: 16 minutes | Serves 4

- ✓ 4 boneless chicken wings
- ✓ 1 tablespoon olive oil
- ✓ 1 teaspoon dried rosemary
- ✓ ½ teaspoon garlic powder
- ✓ ¼ teaspoon salt

Instructions

1. In the mixing bowl, mix up olive oil, dried rosemary, garlic powder, and salt. 2. Then rub the chicken wings with the rosemary mixture and leave for 10 minutes to marinate. 3. After this, put the chicken wings in the instant pot, add the remaining rosemary marinade and cook them on Sauté mode for 8 minutes from each side.

Per Serving:

calories: 222 | fat: 11g | protein: 27g | carbs: 2g | net carbs: 2g | fiber: 0g

Macadamia Nut Cream Cheese Log

Preparation time: 10 minutes | Cook time: 0 minutes | Serves 8

- ✓ 1 (8-ounce / 227-g) brick cream cheese, cold
- ✓ 1 cup finely chopped macadamia nuts

Instructions

1. Place the cream cheese on a piece of parchment paper or wax paper. 2. Roll the paper around the cream cheese, then roll the wrapped cream cheese with the palm of your hands lengthwise on the cream cheese, using the paper to help you roll the cream cheese into an 8-inch log. 3. Open the paper and

sprinkle the macadamia nuts all over the top and sides of the cream cheese until the log is entirely covered in nuts. 4. Chill in the refrigerator for 30 minutes before serving. 5. Serve on a small plate, cut into 8 even slices.

Per Serving:

calories: 285 | fat: 29g | protein: 4g | carbs: 4g | net carbs: 3g | fiber: 1g

Bacon-Wrapped Avocado Fries

Preparation time: 10 minutes | Cook time: 18 minutes | Serves 4

- ✓ 2 medium Hass avocados, peeled and pitted (about 8 oz/220 g of flesh)
- ✓ 16 strips bacon (about 1 lb/455 g), cut in half lengthwise

Instructions

1. Cut each avocado into 8 fry-shaped pieces, making a total of 16 fries. 2. Wrap each avocado fry in 2 half-strips of bacon. Once complete, place in a large frying pan. 3. Set the pan over medium heat and cover with a splash guard. Fry for 6 minutes on each side and on the bottom, or until crispy, for a total of 18 minutes. 4. Remove from the heat and enjoy immediately!

Per Serving:

calories: 723 | fat: 58g | protein: 43g | carbs: 6g | net carbs: 3g | fiber: 4g

Walnut Herb-Crusted Goat Cheese

Preparation time: 10 minutes | Cook time: 0 minutes | Serves 4

- ✓ 6 ounces chopped walnuts
- ✓ 1 tablespoon chopped oregano
- ✓ 1 tablespoon chopped parsley
- ✓ 1 teaspoon chopped fresh thyme
- ✓ ¼ teaspoon freshly ground black pepper
- ✓ 1 (8 ounces) log goat cheese

Instructions

1. Place the walnuts, oregano, parsley, thyme, and pepper in a food processor and pulse until finely chopped. 2. Pour the walnut mixture onto a plate and roll the goat cheese log in the nut mixture,

pressing so the cheese is covered and the walnut mixture sticks to the log. 3. Wrap the cheese in plastic and store in the refrigerator for up to 1 week. 4. Slice and enjoy!

Per Serving:

calories: 304 | fat: 28g | protein: 12g | carbs: 4g | net carbs: 2g | fiber: 2g

Pecan Sandy Fat Bombs

Preparation time: 15 minutes | Cook time: 0 minutes | Makes 8 fat bombs

- ✓ ½ cup (1 stick) unsalted butter, room temperature
- ✓ ¼ cup granulated sugar-free sweetener
- ✓ ½ teaspoon vanilla extract
- ✓ 1 cup almond flour
- ✓ ¾ cup chopped roasted unsalted pecans, divided

Instructions

1. In a large bowl, use an electric mixer on medium speed to cream together the butter and sweetener until smooth. Add the vanilla and beat well. 2. Add the almond flour and ½ cup of chopped pecans, and stir until well incorporated. Place the mixture in the refrigerator for 30 minutes, or until slightly hardened. Meanwhile, very finely chop the remaining ¼ cup of pecans. 3. Using a spoon or your hands, form the chilled mixture into 8 (1-inch) round balls and place on a baking sheet lined with parchment paper. Roll each ball in the finely chopped pecans, and refrigerate for at least 30 minutes before serving. Store in an airtight container in the refrigerator for up to 1 week or in the freezer for up to 2 months.

Per Serving:

calories: 242 | fat: 25g | protein: 4g | carbs: 4g | net carbs: 1g | fiber: 3g

Dairy-Free Queso

Preparation time: 10 minutes | Cook time: 10 minutes | Serves 5

- ✓ 1 cup (130 g) raw cashews
- ✓ ½ cup (120 ml) nondairy milk

- ✓ ¼ cup (17 g) nutritional yeast
- ✓ ½ teaspoon finely ground sea salt
- ✓ ¼ cup (60 ml) avocado oil
- ✓ 1 medium yellow onion, sliced
- ✓ 2 cloves garlic, roughly chopped
- ✓ 1 tablespoon chili powder
- ✓ 1 teaspoon ground cumin
- ✓ ¾ teaspoon garlic powder
- ✓ ¼ teaspoon onion powder
- ✓ ½ teaspoon dried oregano leaves
- ✓ ⅛ teaspoon paprika
- ✓ ⅛ teaspoon cayenne pepper
- ✓ 3½ ounces (100 g) pork rinds, or 2 medium zucchinis, cut into sticks, for serving (optional)

Instructions

1. Place the cashews in a 12-ounce (350-ml) or larger sealable container. Cover with water. Seal and place in the fridge to soak for 12 hours. 2. After 12 hours, drain and rinse the cashews, then place them in a food processor or blender along with the milk, nutritional yeast, and salt. Set aside. 3. Heat the oil in a medium-sized frying pan over medium-low heat until shimmering. Add the onion, garlic, and spices and toss to coat the onion with the seasonings. Stir the mixture every couple of minutes until the onion begins to soften, about 10 minutes. 4. Transfer the onion mixture to the food processor or blender. Cover and blend until smooth. 5. Enjoy the queso with pork rinds or zucchini sticks, if desired.

Per Serving:

calories: 300 | fat: 24g | protein: 7g | carbs: 14g | net carbs: 11g | fiber: 3g

Chinese Spare Ribs

Preparation time: 3 minutes | Cook time: 24 minutes | Serves 6

- ✓ 1½ pounds (680 g) spare ribs
- ✓ Salt and ground black pepper, to taste
- ✓ 2 tablespoons sesame oil
- ✓ ½ cup chopped green onions
- ✓ ½ cup chicken stock
- ✓ 2 tomatoes, crushed
- ✓ 2 tablespoons sherry

- ✓ 1 tablespoon coconut aminos
- ✓ 1 teaspoon ginger-garlic paste
- ✓ ½ teaspoon crushed red pepper flakes
- ✓ ½ teaspoon dried parsley
- ✓ 2 tablespoons sesame seeds, for serving

Instructions

1. Season the spare ribs with salt and black pepper to taste. 2. Set your Instant Pot to Sauté and heat the sesame oil. 3. Add the seasoned spare ribs and sear each side for about 3 minutes. 4. Add the remaining ingredients except the sesame seeds to the Instant Pot and stir well. 5. Secure the lid. Select the Meat/Stew mode and set the cooking time for 18 minutes at High Pressure. 6. When the timer beeps, perform a natural pressure release for 10 minutes, then release any remaining pressure. Carefully remove the lid. 7. Serve topped with the sesame seeds.

Per Serving:

calories: 336 | fat: 16g | protein: 43g | carbs: 3g | net carbs: 2g | fiber: 1g

Pimento Cheese

Preparation time: 20 minutes | Cook time: 0 minutes | serves 8

- ✓ 1 (8-ounce) block sharp cheddar cheese
- ✓ 1 (8-ounce) block mild cheddar cheese
- ✓ 1 cup mayonnaise
- ✓ 1 (4-ounce) jar diced pimentos, drained
- ✓ 3 ounces cream cheese (6 tablespoons), softened
- ✓ 1 tablespoon finely chopped onions
- ✓ 1 tablespoon dill relish
- ✓ ½ teaspoon onion powder
- ✓ ¼ teaspoon garlic powder
- ✓ ¼ teaspoon ground black pepper
- ✓ Serving Suggestions:
- ✓ Sliced bell peppers or celery
- ✓ Pork rinds

Instructions

1. Using the large holes on the side of a box grater, shred the cheeses into a large bowl. 2. Add the rest of the ingredients to the bowl with the shredded cheese

and mix with a spoon until well combined. Refrigerate for at least 1 hour before serving. Leftovers can be stored in an airtight container in the refrigerator for up to a week.

Per Serving:

calories: 464 | fat: 46g | protein: 14g | carbs: 3g | net carbs: 3g | fiber: 0g

Baked Crab Dip

Preparation time: 15 minutes | Cook time: 25 minutes | Serves 4 to 6

- ✓ 4 ounces cream cheese, softened
- ✓ ½ cup shredded Parmesan cheese, plus ½ cup extra for topping (optional) ⅓ cup mayonnaise
- ✓ ¼ cup sour cream
- ✓ 1 tablespoon chopped fresh parsley
- ✓ 2 teaspoons fresh lemon juice
- ✓ 1½ teaspoons Sriracha sauce
- ✓ ½ teaspoon garlic powder
- ✓ 8 ounces fresh lump crabmeat
- ✓ Salt and pepper

Instructions

1. Preheat the oven to 375°F. 2. Combine all the ingredients except for the crabmeat in a mixing bowl and use a hand mixer to blend until smooth. 3. Put the crabmeat in a separate bowl, check for shells, and rinse with cold water, if needed. Pat dry or allow to rest in a strainer until most of the water has drained. 4. Add the crabmeat to the bowl with the cream cheese mixture and gently fold to combine. Taste for seasoning and add salt and pepper to taste, if needed. Pour into an 8-inch round or square baking dish and bake for 25 minutes, until the cheese has melted and the dip is warm throughout. 5. If desired, top the dip with another ½ cup of Parmesan cheese and broil for 2 to 3 minutes, until the cheese has melted and browned slightly.

Per Serving:

calories: 275 | fat: 23g | protein: 16g | carbs: 1g | net carbs: 1g | fiber: 0g

Tapenade

Preparation time: 5 minutes | Cook time: 0 minutes | Serves 2

- ✓ 1 cup pitted black olives
- ✓ 1 cup pitted green olives
- ✓ ¼ cup sun-dried tomatoes in oil, drained
- ✓ 6 fresh basil leaves
- ✓ 1 tablespoon capers
- ✓ 1 tablespoon fresh parsley leaves
- ✓ 2 teaspoons fresh thyme leaves
- ✓ Leaves from 1 sprig fresh oregano
- ✓ 1 clove garlic
- ✓ 1 anchovy fillet
- ✓ ¼ cup olive oil
- ✓ 6 medium celery stalks, cut into sticks, for serving

Instructions

1. Place all the ingredients, except the olive oil and celery sticks, in a blender or food processor. Pulse until roughly chopped. 2. Add the olive oil and pulse a couple more times, just to combine. 3. Transfer to a 16-ounce (475-ml) or larger serving dish and enjoy with celery sticks. Store it: :Keep in an airtight container in the fridge for up to 5 days.

Per Serving:

calories: 167 | fat: 16g | protein: 1g | carbs: 4g | net carbs: 3g | fiber: 1g

Bacon-Pepper Fat Bombs

Preparation time: 10 minutes | Cook time: 0 minutes | Makes 12 fat bombs

- ✓ 2 ounces goat cheese, at room temperature
- ✓ 2 ounces cream cheese, at room temperature
- ✓ ¼ cup butter, at room temperature
- ✓ 8 bacon slices, cooked and chopped
- ✓ Pinch freshly ground black pepper

Instructions

1. Line a small baking sheet with parchment paper and set aside. 2. In a medium bowl, stir together the goat cheese, cream cheese, butter, bacon, and pepper until well combined. 3. Use a tablespoon to drop mounds of the bomb mixture on the baking sheet and place the sheet in the freezer until the fat bombs are very firm but not frozen, about 1 hour. 4. Store the fat bombs in a sealed container in the

refrigerator for up to 2 weeks.

Per Serving:

1 fat bomb: calories: 89 | fat: 8g | protein: 3g | carbs: 0g | net carbs: 0g | fiber: 0g

Lime Brussels Chips

Preparation time: 15 minutes | Cook time: 10 minutes | Serves 2

- ✓ 3 cups Brussels sprouts leaves (from 1½ to 2 pounds fresh Brussels sprouts) Juice of ½ lime
- ✓ 2½ tablespoons avocado oil or melted coconut oil
- ✓ Pink Himalayan salt

Instructions

1. Preheat the oven to 400°F. Line a rimmed baking sheet with parchment paper. 2. Trim off the flat stem ends of the Brussels sprouts and separate the leaves. You should end up with 2 to 3 cups of leaves. 3. Place the separated leaves in a large bowl and add the lime juice. 4. Add the oil and season with salt to taste. Toss until the leaves are evenly coated. 5. Spread the leaves evenly on the prepared baking sheet and bake for 7 to 10 minutes, until lightly golden brown. tip: Trimming a little higher up than usual on the stem end of the Brussels sprouts helps the leaves come off easier.

Per Serving:

calories: 173 | fat: 18g | protein: 2g | carbs: 4g | net carbs: 2g | fiber: 2g

Cookie Fat Bombs

Preparation time: 10 minutes | Cook time: 0 minutes | serves 6

- ✓ 1 cup almond butter
- ✓ ½ cup coconut flour
- ✓ 1 teaspoon ground cinnamon
- ✓ ¼ cup cacao nibs or vegan keto chocolate chips

Instructions

1. Line a baking sheet with parchment paper. If you don't have parchment paper, use aluminum foil or a greased pan. 2. In a mixing bowl, whisk together the almond butter, coconut flour, and cinnamon. 3. Fold in the cacao nibs. 4. Cover the bowl and put it in the

freezer for 15 to 20 minutes. 5. Remove the bowl from the freezer and, using a spoon or cookie scoop, scoop out a dollop of mixture and roll it between your palms to form a ball. Repeat to use all the mixture. 6. Place the fat bombs on a baking sheet and put the sheet in the freezer to chill for 20 minutes until firm.

Per Serving:

calories: 319 | fat: 26g | protein: 8g | carbs: 18g | net carbs: 8g | fiber: 10g

Peanut Butter Keto Fudge

Preparation time: 5 minutes | Cook time: 10 minutes | Serves 12

- ✓ ½ cup (1 stick) butter
- ✓ 8 ounces (227 g) cream cheese
- ✓ 1 cup unsweetened peanut butter
- ✓ 1 teaspoon vanilla extract (or the seeds from 1 vanilla bean)
- ✓ 1 teaspoon liquid stevia (optional)

Instructions

1. Line an 8 or 9-inch square or 9-by-13-inch rectangular baking dish with parchment paper. Set aside. 2. In a saucepan over medium heat, melt the butter and cream cheese together, stirring frequently, for about 5 minutes. 3. Add the peanut butter and continue to stir until smooth. Remove from the heat. 4. Stir in the vanilla and stevia (if using). Pour the mixture into the prepared dish and spread into an even layer. Refrigerate for about 1 hour until thickened and set enough to cut and handle. Cut into small squares and enjoy! Refrigerate, covered, for up to 1 week.

Per Serving:

1 fudge square: calories: 261 | fat: 24g | protein: 8g | carbs: 5g | net carbs: 4g | fiber: 1g

Warm Herbed Olives

Preparation time: 5 minutes | Cook time: 4 minutes | Serves 4

- ✓ ¼ cup good-quality olive oil
- ✓ 4 ounces green olives
- ✓ 4 ounces Kalamata olives

- ✓ ½ teaspoon dried thyme
- ✓ ¼ teaspoon fennel seeds
- ✓ Pinch red pepper flakes

Instructions

1. Sauté the olives. In a large skillet over medium heat, warm the olive oil. Sauté the olives, thyme, fennel seeds, and red pepper flakes until the olives start to brown, 3 to 4 minutes. 2. Serve. Put the olives into a bowl and serve them warm.

Per Serving:

calories: 165 | fat: 17g | protein: 1g | carbs: 3g | net carbs: 2g | fiber: 1g

Keto Taco Shells

Preparation time: 5 minutes | Cook time: 20 minutes | Serves 4

- ✓ 6 ounces (170 g) shredded cheese

Instructions

1. Preheat the oven to 350°F (180°C). 2. Line a baking sheet with a silicone baking mat or parchment paper. 3. Separate the cheese into 4 (1½-ounce / 43-g) portions and make small circular piles a few inches apart (they will spread a bit in the oven). Pat the cheese down so all the piles are equally thick. Bake for 10 to 12 minutes or until the edges begin to brown. Cool for just a couple of minutes. 4. Lay a wooden spoon or spatula across two overturned glasses. Repeat to make a second setup, and carefully transfer a baked cheese circle to drape over the length of each spoon or spatula. Let them cool into the shape of a taco shell. 5. Fill with your choice of protein and top with chopped lettuce, avocado, salsa, sour cream, or whatever else you like on your tacos. These taco shells will keep refrigerated in an airtight container for a few days, but they are best freshly made and still a little warm.

Per Serving:

1 taco shell: calories: 168 | fat: 14g | protein: 11g | carbs: 1g | net carbs: 1g | fiber: 0g

Prosciutto-Wrapped Asparagus

Preparation time: 5 minutes | Cook time: 12 minutes | Serves 6

- ✓ 18 asparagus spears, ends trimmed
- ✓ 2 tablespoons coconut oil, melted
- ✓ 6 slices prosciutto
- ✓ 1 teaspoon garlic powder

Instructions

1. Preheat the oven to 400°F. Line a rimmed baking sheet with parchment paper. 2. Place the asparagus and coconut oil in a large zip-top plastic bag. Seal and toss until the asparagus is evenly coated. 3. Wrap a slice of prosciutto around 3 grouped asparagus spears. Repeat with the remaining prosciutto and asparagus, making a total of 6 bundles. Arrange the bundles in a single layer on the lined baking sheet. Sprinkle the garlic powder over the bundles. 4. Bake for 8 to 12 minutes, until the asparagus is tender.

Per Serving:

calories: 122 | fat: 10g | protein: 8g | carbs: 3g | net carbs: 2g | fiber: 1g

Baked Brie with Pecans

Preparation time: 5 minutes | Cook time: 10 minutes | Serves 6

- ✓ 1 (¾ pound / 340 g) wheel Brie cheese
- ✓ 3 ounces (85 g) pecans, chopped
- ✓ 2 garlic cloves, minced
- ✓ 2 tablespoons minced fresh rosemary leaves
- ✓ 1½ tablespoons olive oil
- ✓ Salt and freshly ground black pepper, to taste

Instructions

1. Preheat the oven to 400°F (205°C). 2. Line a baking sheet with parchment paper and place the Brie on it. 3. In a small bowl, stir together the pecans, garlic, rosemary, and olive oil. Season with salt and pepper. Spoon the mixture in an even layer over the Brie. Bake for about 10 minutes until the cheese is warm and the nuts are lightly browned. 4. Remove and let it cool for 1 to 2 minutes before serving.

Per Serving:

calories: 318 | fat: 29g | protein: 13g | carbs: 3g | net carbs: 2g | fiber: 1g

Southern Pimento Cheese Dip

Preparation time: 5 minutes | Cook time: 0 minutes | Serves 10

- ✓ 8 ounces (227 g) cream cheese, at room temperature
- ✓ 1 cup shredded sharp Cheddar cheese
- ✓ 1 cup shredded Pepper Jack cheese
- ✓ ⅓ cup mayonnaise
- ✓ 1 (4-ounce / 113-g) jar pimentos, diced
- ✓ 1 teaspoon garlic powder
- ✓ 1 teaspoon onion powder
- ✓ ¼ teaspoon cayenne pepper
- ✓ Pinch sea salt
- ✓ Pinch freshly ground black pepper

Instructions

1. In a large bowl, combine the cream cheese, Cheddar, Pepper Jack, mayonnaise, pimentos, garlic powder, onion powder, and cayenne. Beat together using an electric mixer. Season with salt and pepper and beat again until well combined. 2. Chill in the refrigerator for a few hours (or overnight) to let the flavors set.

Per Serving:

calories: 225 | fat: 21g | protein: 7g | carbs: 2g | net carbs: 2g | fiber: 0g

Taco Beef Bites

Preparation time: 10 minutes | Cook time: 15 minutes | Serves 6

- ✓ 10 ounces (283 g) ground beef
- ✓ 3 eggs, beaten
- ✓ ⅓ cup shredded Mozzarella cheese
- ✓ 1 teaspoon taco seasoning
- ✓ 1 teaspoon sesame oil

Instructions

1. In the mixing bowl mix up ground beef, eggs, Mozzarella, and taco seasoning. 2. Then make the small meat bites from the mixture. 3. Heat up sesame oil in the instant pot. 4. Put the meat bites in the hot oil and cook them for 5 minutes from each side on Sauté mode.

Per Serving:

calories: 132 | fat: 6g | protein: 17g | carbs: 1g | net carbs: 1g | fiber: 0g

Garlic Herb Butter

Preparation time: 10 minutes | Cook time: 8 minutes | Serves 4

- ✓ ⅓ cup butter
- ✓ 1 teaspoon dried parsley
- ✓ 1 tablespoon dried dill
- ✓ ½ teaspoon minced garlic
- ✓ ¼ teaspoon dried thyme

Instructions

1. Preheat the instant pot on Sauté mode. 2. Then add butter and melt it. 3. Add dried parsley, dill, minced garlic, and thyme. Stir the butter mixture well. 4. Transfer it in the butter mold and refrigerate until it is solid.

Per Serving:

calories: 138 | fat: 15g | protein: 0g | carbs: 1g | net carbs: 1g | fiber: 0g

Strawberry Shortcake Coconut Ice

Preparation time: 5 minutes | Cook time: 0 minutes | Serves 5

- ✓ 9 hulled strawberries (fresh or frozen and defrosted)
- ✓ ⅓ cup (85 g) coconut cream
- ✓ 1 tablespoon apple cider vinegar
- ✓ 2 drops liquid stevia, or 2 teaspoons erythritol
- ✓ 3 cups (420 g) ice cubes

Instructions

1. Place the strawberries, coconut cream, vinegar, and sweetener in a blender or food processor. Blend until smooth. 2. Add the ice and pulse until crushed. 3. Divide among four ¾-cup (180-ml) or larger bowls and serve immediately.

Per Serving:

calories: 61 | fat: 5g | protein: 0g | carbs: 3g | net carbs: 2g | fiber: 1g

Cauliflower Patties

Preparation time: 10 minutes | Cook time: 10 minutes | Makes 10 patties

- ✓ 1 medium head cauliflower (about 1½

pounds/680 g), or 3 cups (375 g) pre-riced cauliflower

- ✓ 2 large eggs
- ✓ ⅔ cup (75 g) blanched almond flour
- ✓ ¼ cup (17 g) nutritional yeast
- ✓ 1 tablespoon dried chives
- ✓ 1 teaspoon finely ground sea salt
- ✓ 1 teaspoon garlic powder
- ✓ ½ teaspoon turmeric powder
- ✓ ¼ teaspoon ground black pepper
- ✓ 3 tablespoons coconut oil or ghee, for the pan

Instructions

1. If you're using pre-riced cauliflower, skip ahead to Step 2. Otherwise, cut the base off the head of cauliflower and remove the florets. Transfer the florets to a food processor or blender and pulse 3 or 4 times to break them up into small (¼-inch/6-mm) pieces. 2. Transfer the riced cauliflower to a medium-sized saucepan and add enough water to the pan to completely cover the cauliflower. Cover with the lid and bring to a boil over medium heat. Boil, covered, for 3½ minutes. 3. Meanwhile, place a fine-mesh strainer over a bowl. 4. Pour the hot cauliflower into the strainer, allowing the bowl to catch the boiling water. With a spoon, press down on the cauliflower to remove as much water as possible. 5. Discard the cooking water and place the cauliflower in the bowl, then add the eggs, almond flour, nutritional yeast, chives, salt, and spices. Stir until everything is incorporated. 6. Heat a large frying pan over medium-low heat. Add the oil and allow to melt completely. 7. Using a ¼-cup (60-ml) scoop, scoop up a portion of the mixture and roll between your hands to form a ball about 1¾ inches (4.5 cm) in diameter. Place in the hot oil and flatten the ball with the back of a fork until it is a patty about ½ inch (Instructions 1.25 cm) thick. Repeat with the remaining cauliflower mixture, making a total of 10 patties. 8. Cook the patties for 5 minutes per side, or until golden brown. Transfer to a serving plate and enjoy!

Per Serving:

calories: 164 | fat: 12g | protein: 7g | carbs: 7g | net

carbs: 3g | fiber: 4g

Asiago Shishito Peppers

Preparation time: 5 minutes | Cook time: 10 minutes | Serves 4

- ✓ Oil, for spraying
- ✓ 6 ounces (170 g) shishito peppers
- ✓ 1 tablespoon olive oil
- ✓ ½ teaspoon salt
- ✓ ½ teaspoon lemon pepper
- ✓ ⅓ cup grated Asiago cheese, divided

Instructions

1. Line the air fryer basket with parchment and spray lightly with oil. 2. Rinse the shishitos and pat dry with paper towels. 3. In a large bowl, mix together the shishitos, olive oil, salt, and lemon pepper. Place the shishitos in the prepared basket. 4. Roast at 350°F (177°C) for 10 minutes, or until blistered but not burned. 5. Sprinkle with half of the cheese and cook for 1 more minute. 6. Transfer to a serving plate. Immediately sprinkle with the remaining cheese and serve.

Per Serving:

calories: 90 | fat: 6g | protein: 3g | carbs: 7g | net carbs: 6g | fiber: 1g

Herbed Mushrooms

Preparation time: 5 minutes | Cook time: 10 minutes | Serves 4

- ✓ 2 tablespoons butter
- ✓ 2 cloves garlic, minced
- ✓ 20 ounces (567 g) button mushrooms
- ✓ 1 tablespoon coconut aminos
- ✓ 1 teaspoon dried rosemary
- ✓ 1 teaspoon dried basil
- ✓ 1 teaspoon dried sage
- ✓ 1 bay leaf
- ✓ Sea salt, to taste
- ✓ ½ teaspoon freshly ground black pepper
- ✓ ½ cup chicken broth
- ✓ ½ cup water
- ✓ 1 tablespoon roughly chopped fresh parsley leaves, for garnish

Instructions

1. Set your Instant Pot to Sauté and melt the butter. 2. Add the garlic and mushrooms and sauté for 3 to 4 minutes until the garlic is fragrant. 3. Add the remaining ingredients except the parsley to the Instant Pot and stir well. 4. Lock the lid. Select the Manual mode and set the cooking time for 5 minutes at High Pressure. 5. When the timer beeps, perform a quick pressure release. Carefully open the lid. 6. Remove the mushrooms from the pot to a platter. Serve garnished with the fresh parsley leaves.

Per Serving:

calories: 94 | fat: 7g | protein: 6g | carbs: 5g | net carbs: 4g | fiber: 1g

Garlic Meatballs

Preparation time: 20 minutes | Cook time: 15 minutes | Serves 6

- ✓ 7 ounces (198 g) ground beef
- ✓ 7 ounces (198 g) ground pork
- ✓ 1 teaspoon minced garlic
- ✓ 3 tablespoons water
- ✓ 1 teaspoon chili flakes
- ✓ 1 teaspoon dried parsley
- ✓ 1 tablespoon coconut oil
- ✓ ¼ cup beef broth

Instructions

1. In the mixing bowl, mix up ground beef, ground pork, minced garlic, water, chili flakes, and dried parsley. 2. Make the medium size meatballs from the mixture. 3. After this, heat up coconut oil in the instant pot on Sauté mode. 4. Put the meatballs in the hot coconut oil in one layer and cook them for 2 minutes from each side. 5. Then add beef broth and close the lid. 6. Cook the meatballs for 10 minutes on Manual mode (High Pressure). 7. Then make a quick pressure release and transfer the meatballs on the plate.

Per Serving:

calories: 131 | fat: 6g | protein: 19g | carbs: 0g | net carbs: 0g | fiber: 0g

Cheddar Chips

Preparation time: 10 minutes | Cook time: 5 minutes | Serves 4

- ✓ 1 cup shredded Cheddar cheese
- ✓ 1 tablespoon almond flour

Instructions

1. Mix up Cheddar cheese and almond flour. 2. Then preheat the instant pot on Sauté mode. 3. Line the instant pot bowl with baking paper. 4. After this, make the small rounds from the cheese in the instant pot (on the baking paper) and close the lid. 5. Cook them for 5 minutes on Sauté mode or until the cheese is melted. 6. Then switch off the instant pot and remove the baking paper with cheese rounds from it. 7. Cool the chips well and remove them from the baking paper.

Per Serving:

calories: 154 | fat: 13g | protein: 9g | carbs: 2g | net carbs: 1g | fiber: 1g

Herbed Cashew Cheese

Preparation time: 10 minutes | Cook time: 0 minutes | Makes 1½ cups

- ✓ 1 cup raw cashews
- ✓ 1 cup warm water
- ✓ ¼ cup extra-virgin olive oil
- ✓ ¼ cup water
- ✓ 2 tablespoons fresh lemon juice
- ✓ 1 clove garlic, minced or grated
- ✓ 2 tablespoons minced fresh chives
- ✓ Sea salt and ground black pepper, to taste

Instructions

1. Place the cashews in a small container and add the warm water. (If it doesn't cover the cashews completely, just add more warm water.) Soak for 1 to 4 hours unrefrigerated or up to overnight in the refrigerator. 2. Drain and rinse the cashews, then place them in a blender or food processor. Add the olive oil, the ¼ cup water, the lemon juice, and the garlic. Process until smooth and creamy, stopping occasionally to scrape down the sides of the processor, about 5 minutes total. Mix in the chives

and add salt and pepper to taste. 3. If you'd like a lighter texture, add warm water, 1 tablespoon at a time, until you achieve the desired consistency.

Per Serving:

calories: 288 | fat: 25g | protein: 7g | carbs: 13g | net carbs: 12g | fiber: 1g

Cucumber Finger Sandwiches

Preparation time: 10 minutes | Cook time: 0 minutes | serves 4

- ✓ 1 medium English cucumber
- ✓ 2 ounces cream cheese (¼ cup), softened
- ✓ 2 to 3 slices sharp cheddar cheese, cut into 1-inch pieces
- ✓ 4 slices bacon, cooked and cut crosswise into 1-inch pieces

Instructions

1. Slice the cucumber crosswise into rounds about ¼ inch thick. Spread the cream cheese on half of the cucumber slices, then top each with a piece of cheese and a piece of bacon. Place the remainder of the cucumber slices on top to make sandwiches. Serve immediately or cover and refrigerate before serving. These sandwiches should be eaten the day they are made or they will become soggy.

Per Serving:

calories: 187 | fat: 14g | protein: 10g | carbs: 3g | net carbs: 3g | fiber: 0g

Chicken and Cabbage Salad

Preparation time: 15 minutes | Cook time: 10 minutes | Serves 4

- ✓ 12 ounces (340 g) chicken fillet, chopped
- ✓ 1 teaspoon Cajun seasoning
- ✓ 1 tablespoon coconut oil
- ✓ 1 cup chopped Chinese cabbage
- ✓ 1 tablespoon avocado oil
- ✓ 1 teaspoon sesame seeds

Instructions

1. Sprinkle the chopped chicken with the Cajun seasoning. 2. Set your Instant Pot to Sauté and heat the coconut oil. Add the chicken and cook for 10 minutes, stirring occasionally. 3. When the chicken

is cooked, transfer to a salad bowl. Add the cabbage, avocado oil, and sesame seeds and gently toss to combine. Serve immediately.

Per Serving:

calories: 207 | fat: 11g | protein: 25g | carbs: 1g | net carbs: 0g | fiber: 0g

Hot Chard Artichoke Dip

Preparation time: 10 minutes | Cook time: 20 minutes | Serves 4

- ✓ 4 ounces cream cheese, at room temperature
- ✓ ½ cup coconut milk
- ✓ ½ cup grated Asiago cheese
- ✓ ½ cup shredded Cheddar cheese
- ✓ 1 teaspoon minced garlic
- ✓ Dash hot sauce (optional)
- ✓ 2 cups chopped Swiss chard
- ✓ ¼ cup roughly chopped artichoke hearts (packed in brine, not oil)

Instructions

1. Preheat the oven. Set the oven temperature to 450°F. 2. Mix the ingredients. In a large bowl, stir together the cream cheese, coconut milk, Asiago, Cheddar, garlic, and hot sauce (if using), until everything is well mixed. Stir in the chard and the artichoke hearts and mix until they're well incorporated. Note: You've got to use artichokes packed in brine rather than oil because the extra oil will come out of the dip when you heat it, which will mess up the texture. 3. Bake. Spoon the mixture into a 1-quart baking dish, and bake it for 15 to 20 minutes until it's bubbly and lightly golden. 4. Serve. Cut up low-carb veggies to serve with this creamy, rich dip.

Per Serving:

calories: 280 | fat: 25g | protein: 11g | carbs: 5g | net carbs: 4g | fiber: 1g

Crab Stuffed Mushrooms

Preparation time: 10 minutes | Cook time: 20 minutes | Serves 4

- ✓ 1 cup cooked chopped crab
- ✓ 1 cup cream cheese, softened

- ✓ ½ cup grated Parmesan cheese
- ✓ ¼ cup ground almonds
- ✓ 1 scallion, chopped
- ✓ 1 tablespoon chopped fresh parsley
- ✓ 1 teaspoon minced garlic
- ✓ 12 large button mushrooms, cleaned and stemmed
- ✓ Olive oil cooking spray

Instructions

1. Preheat the oven. Set the oven temperature to 375°F. Line a baking sheet with parchment paper. 2. Mix the filling. In a large bowl, stir together the crab, cream cheese, Parmesan, almonds, scallion, parsley, and garlic until everything is well mixed. 3. Precook the mushrooms. Place the mushrooms stem-side up on the baking sheet and lightly spray them with olive oil. Bake them for 2 minutes then drain them stem-side down on paper towels. 4. Stuff the mushrooms. Turn the mushrooms over and place them back on the baking sheet. Spoon about 1½ tablespoons of the filling into each mushroom. 5. Bake the mushrooms. Bake for 15 minutes until the mushrooms are lightly golden and bubbly. 6. Serve. Arrange the mushrooms on a serving platter.

Per Serving:

calories: 300 | fat: 25g | protein: 16g | carbs: 4g | net carbs: 4g | fiber: 0g

Snappy Bacon Asparagus

Preparation time: 20 minutes | Cook time: 25 minutes | Serves 6

- ✓ 24 asparagus spears
- ✓ 6 strips no-sugar-added bacon, uncooked
- ✓ 2 tablespoons olive oil
- ✓ ⅛ teaspoon salt

Instructions

1. My favorite part of preparing asparagus is the SNAP. Grab the "nonpointed" end of stalk and bend until it breaks. This usually happens about an inch from the end with the cut. Now, line up asparagus and cut entire bunch at "snapping" point, making all of your stalks uniform in length. Fancy, right? 2. On a microwave-safe plate, microwave asparagus 2 minutes to soften. Let cool 5 minutes. 3. Lay strip of bacon on a cutting board at 45-degree angle. Lay four asparagus spears centered on bacon in an "up and down" position. 4. Pick up bacon and asparagus where they meet and wrap two ends of bacon around asparagus in opposite directions. 5. Wrap bacon tightly and secure, pinning bacon to asparagus at ends with toothpicks. Don't worry if bacon doesn't cover entire spears. 6. Brush asparagus with olive oil and sprinkle with salt. 7. Heat a medium nonstick skillet over medium heat. Cook asparagus/bacon 3–5 minutes per side while turning to cook thoroughly. Continue flipping until bacon is brown and crispy.

Per Serving:

calories: 90 | fat: 7g | protein: 5g | carbs: 3g | net carbs: 3g | fiber: 1g

Herbed Zucchini Slices

Preparation time: 5 minutes | Cook time: 5 minutes | Serves 4

- ✓ 2 tablespoons olive oil
- ✓ 2 garlic cloves, chopped
- ✓ 1 pound (454 g) zucchini, sliced
- ✓ ½ cup water
- ✓ ½ cup sugar-free tomato purée
- ✓ 1 teaspoon dried thyme
- ✓ ½ teaspoon dried rosemary
- ✓ ½ teaspoon dried oregano

Instructions

1. Set your Instant Pot to Sauté and heat the olive oil. 2. Add the garlic and sauté for 2 minutes until fragrant. 3. Add the remaining ingredients to the Instant Pot and stir well. 4. Lock the lid. Select the Manual mode and set the cooking time for 3 minutes at Low Pressure. 5. When the timer beeps, perform a quick pressure release. Carefully remove the lid. 6. Serve warm.

Per Serving:

calories: 87 | fat: 8g | protein: 2g | carbs: 5g | net carbs: 3g | fiber: 2g

Crab Salad-Stuffed Avocado

Preparation time: 20 minutes | Cook time: 0

minutes | Serves 2

- ✓ 1 avocado, peeled, halved lengthwise, and pitted
- ✓ ½ teaspoon freshly squeezed lemon juice
- ✓ 4½ ounces Dungeness crabmeat
- ✓ ½ cup cream cheese
- ✓ ¼ cup chopped red bell pepper
- ✓ ¼ cup chopped, peeled English cucumber
- ✓ ½ scallion, chopped
- ✓ 1 teaspoon chopped cilantro
- ✓ Pinch sea salt
- ✓ Freshly ground black pepper

Instructions

1. Brush the cut edges of the avocado with the lemon juice and set the halves aside on a plate. 2. In a medium bowl, stir together the crabmeat, cream cheese, red pepper, cucumber, scallion, cilantro, salt, and pepper until well mixed. 3. Divide the crab mixture between the avocado halves and store them, covered with plastic wrap, in the refrigerator until you want to serve them, up to 2 days.

Per Serving:

calories: 389 | fat: 31g | protein: 19g | carbs: 10g | net carbs: 5g | fiber: 5g

Cubed Tofu Fries

Preparation time: 25 minutes | Cook time: 20

minutes | Serves 4

- ✓ 1 (12 ounces) package extra-firm tofu
- ✓ 2 tablespoons sesame oil
- ✓ ⅛ teaspoon salt, divided
- ✓ ⅛ teaspoon black pepper, divided
- ✓ ⅛ teaspoon creole seasoning, divided

Instructions

1. Remove tofu from packaging and wrap in paper towel. Set on a clean plate. Place a second plate on top and put a 3- to 5-pound weight on top. Let sit 20 minutes. Drain excess water. 2. Unwrap tofu and slice into small cubes no larger than ½" square (a little larger than sugar cubes). 3. In a large skillet over medium heat, heat oil. 4. Combine salt, pepper, and creole seasoning in a small bowl. Sprinkle one-third of spice mixture evenly into skillet and add tofu evenly. 5. Sprinkle one-third of spices on top and let fry 5 minutes on each side, flipping three times (for the four sides), browning all four sides. 6. Dust tofu with remaining spice mixture. 7. Remove from heat. Enjoy while hot!

Per Serving:

calories: 160 | fat: 13g | protein: 8g | carbs: 2g | net carbs: 2g | fiber: 0g

CHAPTER 6 Vegetarian Mains

Broccoli-Cheese Fritters

Preparation time: 5 minutes | Cook time: 20 to 25 minutes | Serves 4

- ✓ 1 cup broccoli florets
- ✓ 1 cup shredded Mozzarella cheese
- ✓ ¾ cup almond flour
- ✓ ½ cup flaxseed meal, divided
- ✓ 2 teaspoons baking powder
- ✓ 1 teaspoon garlic powder
- ✓ Salt and freshly ground black pepper, to taste
- ✓ 2 eggs, lightly beaten
- ✓ ½ cup ranch dressing

Instructions

1. Preheat the air fryer to 400°F (204°C). 2. In a food processor fitted with a metal blade, pulse the broccoli until very finely chopped. 3. Transfer the broccoli to a large bowl and add the Mozzarella, almond flour, ¼ cup of the flaxseed meal, baking powder, and garlic powder. Stir until thoroughly combined. Season to taste with salt and black pepper. Add the eggs and stir again to form a sticky dough. Shape the dough into 1¼-inch fritters. 4. Place the remaining ¼ cup flaxseed meal in a shallow bowl and roll the fritters in the meal to form an even coating. 5. Working in batches if necessary, arrange the fritters in a single layer in the basket of the air fryer and spray generously with olive oil. Pausing halfway through the cooking time to shake the basket, air fry for 20 to 25 minutes until the fritters are golden brown and crispy. Serve with the ranch dressing for dipping.

Per Serving:

calories: 638 | fat: 54g | protein: 28g | carbs: 16g | net carbs: 9g | fiber: 7g

Basic Spaghetti Squash

Preparation time: 10 minutes | Cook time: 45 minutes | Serves 2

- ✓ ½ large spaghetti squash
- ✓ 1 tablespoon coconut oil
- ✓ 2 tablespoons salted butter, melted
- ✓ ½ teaspoon garlic powder
- ✓ 1 teaspoon dried parsley

Instructions

1. Brush shell of spaghetti squash with coconut oil. Place the skin side down and brush the inside with butter. Sprinkle with garlic powder and parsley. 2. Place squash with the skin side down into the air fryer basket. 3. Adjust the temperature to 350°F (177°C) and air fry for 30 minutes. 4. Flip the squash so skin side is up and cook an additional 15 minutes or until fork tender. Serve warm.

Per Serving:

calories: 180 | fat: 17g | protein: 1g | carbs: 8g | net carbs: 5g | fiber: 3g

Cheesy Cauliflower Pizza Crust

Preparation time: 15 minutes | Cook time: 11 minutes | Serves 2

- ✓ 1 (12 ounces / 340 g) steamer bag cauliflower
- ✓ ½ cup shredded sharp Cheddar cheese
- ✓ 1 large egg
- ✓ 2 tablespoons blanched finely ground almond flour
- ✓ 1 teaspoon Italian blend seasoning

Instructions

1. Cook cauliflower according to package instructions. Remove from bag and place into cheesecloth or paper towel to remove excess water. Place cauliflower into a large bowl. 2. Add cheese, egg, almond flour, and Italian seasoning to the bowl and mix well. 3. Cut a piece of parchment to fit your air fryer basket. Press cauliflower into 6-inch round circle. Place into the air fryer basket. 4. Adjust the temperature to 360°F (182°C) and air fry for 11 minutes. 5. After 7 minutes, flip the pizza crust. 6. Add preferred toppings to pizza. Place back into air

fryer basket and cook an additional 4 minutes or until fully cooked and golden. Serve immediately.

Per Serving:

calories: 248 | fat: 18g | protein: 16g | carbs: 8g | net carbs: 4g | fiber: 4g

Zucchini Roll Manicotti

Preparation time: 15 minutes | Cook time: 30 minutes | Serves 4

- ✓ Olive oil cooking spray
- ✓ 4 zucchini
- ✓ 2 tablespoons good-quality olive oil
- ✓ 1 red bell pepper, diced
- ✓ ½ onion, minced
- ✓ 2 teaspoons minced garlic
- ✓ 1 cup goat cheese
- ✓ 1 cup shredded mozzarella cheese
- ✓ 1 tablespoon chopped fresh oregano
- ✓ Sea salt, for seasoning
- ✓ Freshly ground black pepper, for seasoning
- ✓ 2 cups low-carb marinara sauce, divided
- ✓ ½ cup grated Parmesan cheese

Instructions

1. Preheat the oven. Set the oven temperature to 375°F. Lightly grease a 9-by-13-inch baking dish with olive oil cooking spray. 2. Prepare the zucchini. Cut the zucchini lengthwise into ⅛-inch-thick slices and set them aside. 3. Make the filling. In a medium skillet over medium-high heat, warm the olive oil. Add the red bell pepper, onion, and garlic and sauté until they've softened, about 4 minutes. Remove the skillet from the heat and transfer the vegetables to a medium bowl. Stir the goat cheese, mozzarella, and oregano into the vegetables. Season it all with salt and pepper. 4. Assemble the manicotti. Spread 1 cup of the marinara sauce in the bottom of the baking dish. Lay a zucchini slice on a clean cutting board and place a couple tablespoons of filling at one end. Roll the slice up and place it in the baking dish, seam-side down. Repeat with the remaining zucchini slices. Spoon the remaining sauce over the rolls and top with the Parmesan. 5. Bake. Bake the rolls for 30 to 35 minutes until the zucchini is tender and the

cheese is golden. 6. Serve. Spoon the rolls onto four plates and serve them hot.

Per Serving:

calories: 342 | fat: 24g | protein: 20g | carbs: 14g | net carbs: 11g | fiber: 3g

Crispy Cabbage Steaks

Preparation time: 5 minutes | Cook time: 10 minutes | Serves 4

- ✓ 1 small head green cabbage, cored and cut into ½-inch-thick slices
- ✓ ¼ teaspoon salt
- ✓ ¼ teaspoon ground black pepper
- ✓ 2 tablespoons olive oil
- ✓ 1 clove garlic, peeled and finely minced
- ✓ ½ teaspoon dried thyme
- ✓ ½ teaspoon dried parsley

Instructions

1. Sprinkle each side of cabbage with salt and pepper, then place into ungreased air fryer basket, working in batches if needed. 2. Drizzle each side of cabbage with olive oil, then sprinkle with remaining ingredients on both sides. Adjust the temperature to 350°F (177°C) and air fry for 10 minutes, turning "steaks" halfway through cooking. 3.Cabbage will be browned at the edges and tender when done. Serve warm.

Per Serving:

calories: 80 | fat:7g | protein: 1g | carbs: 5g | net carbs: 4g | fiber: 1g

Vegetable Vodka Sauce Bake

Preparation time: 10 minutes | Cook time: 30 minutes | Serves 4

- ✓ 3 tablespoons melted grass-fed butter, divided
- ✓ 4 cups mushrooms, halved
- ✓ 4 cups cooked cauliflower florets
- ✓ 1½ cups purchased vodka sauce
- ✓ ¾ cup heavy (whipping) cream
- ✓ ½ cup grated Asiago cheese
- ✓ Sea salt, for seasoning
- ✓ Freshly ground black pepper, for seasoning
- ✓ 1 cup shredded provolone cheese

✓ 2 tablespoons chopped fresh oregano

Instructions

1. Preheat the oven. Set the oven temperature to 350°F and use 1 tablespoon of the melted butter to grease a 9-by-13-inch baking dish. 2. Mix the vegetables. In a large bowl, combine the mushrooms, cauliflower, vodka sauce, cream, Asiago, and the remaining 2 tablespoons of butter. Season the vegetables with salt and pepper. 3. Bake. Transfer the vegetable mixture to the baking dish and top it with the provolone cheese. Bake for 30 to 35 minutes until it's bubbly and heated through. 4. Serve. Divide the mixture between four plates and top with the oregano.

Per Serving:

calories: 537 | fat: 45g | protein: 19g | carbs: 14g | net carbs: 8g | fiber: 19g

Garlic White Zucchini Rolls

Preparation time: 20 minutes | Cook time: 20 minutes | Serves 4

✓ 2 medium zucchini
✓ 2 tablespoons unsalted butter
✓ ¼ white onion, peeled and diced
✓ ½ teaspoon finely minced roasted garlic
✓ ¼ cup heavy cream
✓ 2 tablespoons vegetable broth
✓ ⅛ teaspoon xanthan gum
✓ ½ cup full-fat ricotta cheese
✓ ¼ teaspoon salt
✓ ½ teaspoon garlic powder
✓ ¼ teaspoon dried oregano
✓ 2 cups spinach, chopped
✓ ½ cup sliced baby portobello mushrooms
✓ ¾ cup shredded Mozzarella cheese, divided

Instructions

1. Using a mandoline or sharp knife, slice zucchini into long strips lengthwise. Place strips between paper towels to absorb moisture. Set aside. 2. In a medium saucepan over medium heat, melt butter. Add onion and sauté until fragrant. Add garlic and sauté 30 seconds. 3. Pour in heavy cream, broth, and xanthan gum. Turn off heat and whisk mixture until it begins to thicken, about 3 minutes. 4. In a medium bowl, add ricotta, salt, garlic powder, and oregano and mix well. Fold in spinach, mushrooms, and ½ cup Mozzarella. 5. Pour half of the sauce into a round baking pan. To assemble the rolls, place two strips of zucchini on a work surface. Spoon 2 tablespoons of ricotta mixture onto the slices and roll up. Place seam side down on top of sauce. Repeat with remaining ingredients. 6. Pour remaining sauce over the rolls and sprinkle with remaining Mozzarella. Cover with foil and place into the air fryer basket. 7. Adjust the temperature to 350°F (177°C) and bake for 20 minutes. 8. In the last 5 minutes, remove the foil to brown the cheese. Serve immediately.

Per Serving:

calories: 270 | fat: 21g | protein: 14g | carbs: 7g | net carbs: 5g | fiber: 2g

Zucchini and Spinach Croquettes

Preparation time: 9 minutes | Cook time: 7 minutes | Serves 6

✓ 4 eggs, slightly beaten
✓ ½ cup almond flour
✓ ½ cup goat cheese, crumbled
✓ 1 teaspoon fine sea salt
✓ 4 garlic cloves, minced
✓ 1 cup baby spinach
✓ ½ cup Parmesan cheese, grated
✓ ⅓ teaspoon red pepper flakes
✓ 1 pound (454 g) zucchini, peeled and grated
✓ ⅓ teaspoon dried dill weed

Instructions

1. Thoroughly combine all ingredients in a bowl. Now, roll the mixture to form small croquettes. 2. Air fry at 340°F (171°C) for 7 minutes or until golden. Tate, adjust for seasonings and serve warm.

Per Serving:

calories: 179 | fat: 12g | protein: 11g | carbs: 6g | net carbs: 3g | fiber: 3g

Green Vegetable Stir-Fry with Tofu

Preparation time: 15 minutes | Cook time: 15 minutes | Serves 2

- ✓ 3 tablespoons avocado oil, divided
- ✓ 1 cup Brussels sprouts, halved
- ✓ ½ onion, diced
- ✓ ½ leek, white and light green parts diced
- ✓ ½ head green cabbage, diced
- ✓ ¼ cup water, plus more if needed
- ✓ ½ cup kale, coarsely chopped
- ✓ 1 cup spinach, coarsely chopped
- ✓ 8 ounces (227 g) tofu, diced
- ✓ 2 teaspoons garlic powder
- ✓ Salt and freshly ground black pepper, to taste
- ✓ ½ avocado, pitted, peeled, and diced
- ✓ MCT oil (optional)

Instructions

1. In a large skillet with a lid (or a wok if you have one), heat 2 tablespoons of avocado oil over medium-high heat. Add the Brussels sprouts, onion, leek, and cabbage and stir together. Add the water, cover, lower the heat to medium, and cook for about 5 minutes. 2. Toss in the kale and spinach and cook for 3 minutes, stirring constantly, until the onion, leek, and cabbage are caramelized. 3. Add the tofu to the stir-fry, then season with the garlic, salt, pepper, and the remaining tablespoon of avocado oil. 4. Turn the heat back up to medium-high and cook for about 10 minutes, stirring constantly, until the tofu is nice and caramelized on all sides. If you experience any burning, turn down the heat and add 2 to 3 tablespoons of water. 5. Divide the stir-fry between two plates and sprinkle with diced avocado. Feel free to drizzle algae oil or MCT oil over the top for a little extra fat.

Per Serving:

calories: 473 | fat: 33g | protein: 17g | carbs: 27g | net carbs: 15g | fiber: 12g

Broccoli with Garlic Sauce

Preparation time: 19 minutes | Cook time: 15 minutes | Serves 4

- ✓ 2 tablespoons olive oil
- ✓ Kosher salt and freshly ground black pepper, to taste
- ✓ 1 pound (454 g) broccoli florets

- ✓ Dipping Sauce:
- ✓ 2 teaspoons dried rosemary, crushed
- ✓ 3 garlic cloves, minced
- ✓ ⅓ teaspoon dried marjoram, crushed
- ✓ ¼ cup sour cream
- ✓ ⅓ cup mayonnaise

Instructions

1. Lightly grease your broccoli with a thin layer of olive oil. Season with salt and ground black pepper. 2. Arrange the seasoned broccoli in the air fryer basket. Bake at 395°F (202°C) for 15 minutes, shaking once or twice. In the meantime, prepare the dipping sauce by mixing all the sauce ingredients. Serve warm broccoli with the dipping sauce and enjoy!

Per Serving:

calories: 250 | fat: 23g | protein: 3g | carbs: 10g | net carbs: 9g | fiber: 1g

Crustless Spanakopita

Preparation time: 15 minutes | Cook time: 45 minutes | Serves 6

- ✓ 12 tablespoons extra-virgin olive oil, divided
- ✓ 1 small yellow onion, diced
- ✓ 1 (32-ounce / 907-g) bag frozen chopped spinach, thawed, fully drained, and patted dry (about 4 cups)
- ✓ 4 garlic cloves, minced
- ✓ ½ teaspoon salt
- ✓ ½ teaspoon freshly ground black pepper
- ✓ 1 cup whole-milk ricotta cheese
- ✓ 4 large eggs
- ✓ ¾ cup crumbled traditional feta cheese
- ✓ ¼ cup pine nuts

Instructions

1. Preheat the oven to 375°F (190°C). 2. In a large skillet, heat 4 tablespoons olive oil over medium-high heat. Add the onion and sauté until softened, 6 to 8 minutes. 3. Add the spinach, garlic, salt, and pepper and sauté another 5 minutes. Remove from the heat and allow to cool slightly. 4. In a medium bowl, whisk together the ricotta and eggs. Add to the cooled spinach and stir to combine. 5. Pour 4 tablespoons olive oil in the bottom of a

9-by-13-inch glass baking dish and swirl to coat the bottom and sides. Add the spinach-ricotta mixture and spread into an even layer. 6. Bake for 20 minutes or until the mixture begins to set. Remove from the oven and crumble the feta evenly across the top of the spinach. Add the pine nuts and drizzle with the remaining 4 tablespoons olive oil. Return to the oven and bake for an additional 15 to 20 minutes, or until the spinach is fully set and the top is starting to turn golden brown. Allow to cool slightly before cutting to serve.

Per Serving:

calories: 440 | fat: 38g | protein: 17g | carbs: 9g | net carbs: 8g | fiber: 1g

Pesto Vegetable Skewers

Preparation time: 30 minutes | Cook time: 8 minutes | Makes 8 skewers

- ✓ 1 medium zucchini, trimmed and cut into ½-inch slices
- ✓ ½ medium yellow onion, peeled and cut into 1-inch squares
- ✓ 1 medium red bell pepper, seeded and cut into 1-inch squares
- ✓ 16 whole cremini mushrooms
- ✓ ⅓ cup basil pesto
- ✓ ½ teaspoon salt
- ✓ ¼ teaspoon ground black pepper

Instructions

1. Divide zucchini slices, onion, and bell pepper into eight even portions. Place on 6-inch skewers for a total of eight kebabs. Add 2 mushrooms to each skewer and brush kebabs generously with pesto. 2. Sprinkle each kebab with salt and black pepper on all sides, then place into ungreased air fryer basket. Adjust the temperature to 375°F (191°C) and air fry for 8 minutes, turning kebabs halfway through cooking. Vegetables will be browned at the edges and tender-crisp when done. Serve warm.

Per Serving:

calories: 50 | fat: 4g | protein: 2g | carbs: 4g | net carbs: 3g | fiber: 1g

Stuffed Eggplant

Preparation time: 20 minutes | Cook time: 1 hour | Serves 2 to 4

- ✓ 1 small eggplant, halved lengthwise
- ✓ 3 tablespoons olive, avocado, or macadamia nut oil
- ✓ 1 onion, diced
- ✓ 12 asparagus spears or green beans, diced
- ✓ 1 red bell pepper, diced
- ✓ 1 large tomato, chopped
- ✓ 2 garlic cloves, minced
- ✓ ½ block (8 ounces / 227 g) extra-firm tofu (optional)
- ✓ 3 tablespoons chopped fresh basil leaves
- ✓ Salt and freshly ground black pepper, to taste
- ✓ ¼ cup water
- ✓ 2 eggs
- ✓ Chopped fresh parsley, for garnish (optional)
- ✓ Shredded cheese, for garnish (optional)

Instructions

1. Preheat the oven to 350°F (180°C). 2. Scoop out the flesh from the halved eggplant and chop it into cubes. Reserve the eggplant skin. 3. In a sauté pan with a lid, heat the oil over medium-high heat. Add the eggplant, onion, asparagus, bell pepper, tomato, garlic, and tofu (if using) and stir. Stir in the basil, season with salt and pepper, and cook for about 5 minutes. 4. Add the water, cover the pan, reduce the heat to medium, and cook for about 15 minutes longer. 5. Put the eggplant "boats" (the reserved skin) on a baking sheet. Scoop some of the cooked eggplant mixture into each boat (you may have some filling left over, which is fine—you can roast it alongside the eggplant). 6. Crack an egg into each eggplant boat, on top of the filling, then bake for about 40 minutes, or until desired doneness. 7. Remove the eggplant from the oven and, if desired, sprinkle parsley and cheese over the top. Let the cheese melt and cool for about 5 minutes, then serve them up!

Per Serving:

calories: 380 | fat: 26g | protein: 12g | carbs: 25g |

net carbs: 15g | fiber: 10g

Sweet Pepper Nachos

Preparation time: 10 minutes | Cook time: 5 minutes | Serves 2

✓ 6 mini sweet peppers, seeded and sliced in half
✓ ¾ cup shredded Colby jack cheese
✓ ¼ cup sliced pickled jalapeños
✓ ½ medium avocado, peeled, pitted, and diced
✓ 2 tablespoons sour cream

Instructions

1. Place peppers into an ungreased round nonstick baking dish. Sprinkle with Colby and top with jalapeños. 2. Place dish into air fryer basket. Adjust the temperature to 350°F (177°C) and bake for 5 minutes. Cheese will be melted and bubbly when done. 3. Remove dish from air fryer and top with avocado. Drizzle with sour cream. Serve warm.

Per Serving:

calories: 255 | fat: 21g | protein: 11g | carbs: 9g | net carbs: 5g | fiber: 4g

Eggplant and Zucchini Bites

Preparation time: 30 minutes | Cook time: 30 minutes | Serves 8

✓ 2 teaspoons fresh mint leaves, chopped
✓ 1½ teaspoons red pepper chili flakes
✓ 2 tablespoons melted butter
✓ 1 pound (454 g) eggplant, peeled and cubed
✓ 1 pound (454 g) zucchini, peeled and cubed
✓ 3 tablespoons olive oil

Instructions

1. Toss all the above ingredients in a large-sized mixing dish. 2. Roast the eggplant and zucchini bites for 30 minutes at 325°F (163°C) in your air fryer, turning once or twice. 3. Serve with a homemade dipping sauce.

Per Serving:

calories: 140 | fat: 12g | protein: 2g | carbs: 8g | net carbs: 6g | fiber: 2g

Quiche-Stuffed Peppers

Preparation time: 5 minutes | Cook time: 15 minutes | Serves 2

✓ 2 medium green bell peppers
✓ 3 large eggs
✓ ¼ cup full-fat ricotta cheese
✓ ¼ cup diced yellow onion
✓ ½ cup chopped broccoli
✓ ½ cup shredded medium Cheddar cheese

Instructions

1. Cut the tops off of the peppers and remove the seeds and white membranes with a small knife. 2. In a medium bowl, whisk eggs and ricotta. 3. Add onion and broccoli. Pour the egg and vegetable mixture evenly into each pepper. Top with Cheddar. Place peppers into a 4-cup round baking dish and place into the air fryer basket. 4. Adjust the temperature to 350°F (177°C) and bake for 15 minutes. 5. Eggs will be mostly firm and peppers tender when fully cooked. Serve immediately.

Per Serving:

calories: 382 | fat: 27g | protein: 24g | carbs: 11g | net carbs: 7g | fiber: 4g

Spinach Cheese Casserole

Preparation time: 15 minutes | Cook time: 15 minutes | Serves 4

✓ 1 tablespoon salted butter, melted
✓ ¼ cup diced yellow onion
✓ 8 ounces (227 g) full-fat cream cheese, softened
✓ ⅓ cup full-fat mayonnaise
✓ ⅓ cup full-fat sour cream
✓ ¼ cup chopped pickled jalapeños
✓ 2 cups fresh spinach, chopped
✓ 2 cups cauliflower florets, chopped
✓ 1 cup artichoke hearts, chopped

Instructions

1. In a large bowl, mix butter, onion, cream cheese, mayonnaise, and sour cream. Fold in jalapeños, spinach, cauliflower, and artichokes. 2. Pour the mixture into a round baking dish. Cover with foil and place into the air fryer basket. 3. Adjust the temperature to 370°F (188°C) and set the timer for 15 minutes. In the last 2 minutes of cooking, remove the foil to brown the top. Serve warm.

Per Serving:

calories: 490 | fat: 46g | protein: 9g | carbs: 12g | net carbs: 8g | fiber: 4g

Spaghetti Squash Alfredo

Preparation time: 10 minutes | Cook time: 15 minutes | Serves 2

- ✓   ½ large cooked spaghetti squash
- ✓   2 tablespoons salted butter, melted
- ✓   ½ cup low-carb Alfredo sauce
- ✓   ¼ cup grated vegetarian Parmesan cheese
- ✓   ½ teaspoon garlic powder
- ✓   1 teaspoon dried parsley
- ✓   ¼ teaspoon ground peppercorn
- ✓   ½ cup shredded Italian blend cheese

Instructions

1. Using a fork, remove the strands of spaghetti squash from the shell. Place into a large bowl with butter and Alfredo sauce. Sprinkle with Parmesan, garlic powder, parsley, and peppercorn. 2. Pour into a 4-cup round baking dish and top with shredded cheese. Place dish into the air fryer basket. 3. Adjust the temperature to 320°F (160°C) and bake for 15 minutes. When finished, cheese will be golden and bubbling. Serve immediately.

Per Serving:

calories: 383 | fat: 30g | protein: 14g | carbs: 14g | net carbs: 11g | fiber: 3g

Crispy Eggplant Rounds

Preparation time: 15 minutes | Cook time: 10 minutes | Serves 4

- ✓   1 large eggplant, ends trimmed, cut into ½-inch slices
- ✓   ½ teaspoon salt
- ✓   2 ounces (57 g) Parmesan 100% cheese crisps, finely ground
- ✓   ½ teaspoon paprika
- ✓   ¼ teaspoon garlic powder
- ✓   1 large egg

Instructions

1. Sprinkle eggplant rounds with salt. Place rounds on a kitchen towel for 30 minutes to draw out excess water. Pat rounds dry. 2. In a medium bowl, mix cheese crisps, paprika, and garlic powder. In a separate medium bowl, whisk egg. Dip each eggplant round in egg, then gently press into cheese crisps to coat both sides. 3. Place eggplant rounds into ungreased air fryer basket. Adjust the temperature to 400°F (204°C) and air fry for 10 minutes, turning rounds halfway through cooking. Eggplant will be golden and crispy when done. Serve warm.

Per Serving:

calories: 133 | fat: 8g | protein: 10g | carbs: 6g | net carbs: 4g | fiber: 3g

Parmesan Artichokes

Preparation time: 10 minutes | Cook time: 10 minutes | Serves 4

- ✓   2 medium artichokes, trimmed and quartered, center removed
- ✓   2 tablespoons coconut oil
- ✓   1 large egg, beaten
- ✓   ½ cup grated vegetarian Parmesan cheese
- ✓   ¼ cup blanched finely ground almond flour
- ✓   ½ teaspoon crushed red pepper flakes

Instructions

1. In a large bowl, toss artichokes in coconut oil and then dip each piece into the egg. 2. Mix the Parmesan and almond flour in a large bowl. Add artichoke pieces and toss to cover as completely as possible, sprinkle with pepper flakes. Place into the air fryer basket. 3. Adjust the temperature to 400°F (204°C) and air fry for 10 minutes. 4. Toss the basket two times during cooking. Serve warm.

Per Serving:

calories: 220 | fat: 18g | protein: 10g | carbs: 9g | net carbs: 4g | fiber: 5g

Loaded Cauliflower Steak

Preparation time: 5 minutes | Cook time: 7 minutes | Serves 4

- ✓   1 medium head cauliflower
- ✓   ¼ cup hot sauce
- ✓   2 tablespoons salted butter, melted
- ✓   ¼ cup blue cheese crumbles
- ✓   ¼ cup full-fat ranch dressing

Instructions

1. Remove cauliflower leaves. Slice the head in ½-inch-thick slices. 2. In a small bowl, mix hot sauce and butter. Brush the mixture over the cauliflower. 3. Place each cauliflower steak into the air fryer, working in batches if necessary. 4. Adjust the temperature to 400°F (204°C) and air fry for 7 minutes. 5. When cooked, edges will begin turning dark and caramelized. 6. To serve, sprinkle steaks with crumbled blue cheese. Drizzle with ranch dressing.

Per Serving:

calories: 140 | fat: 12g | protein: 5g | carbs: 6g | net carbs: 5g | fiber: 1g

Almond-Cauliflower Gnocchi

Preparation time: 5 minutes | Cook time: 25 to 30 minutes | Serves 4

- ✓ 5 cups cauliflower florets
- ✓ ⅔ cup almond flour
- ✓ ½ teaspoon salt
- ✓ ¼ cup unsalted butter, melted
- ✓ ¼ cup grated Parmesan cheese

Instructions

1. In a food processor fitted with a metal blade, pulse the cauliflower until finely chopped. Transfer the cauliflower to a large microwave-safe bowl and cover it with a paper towel. Microwave for 5 minutes. Spread the cauliflower on a towel to cool. 2. When cool enough to handle, draw up the sides of the towel and squeeze tightly over a sink to remove the excess moisture. Return the cauliflower to the food processor and whirl until creamy. Sprinkle in the flour and salt and pulse until a sticky dough comes together. 3. Transfer the dough to a workspace lightly floured with almond flour. Shape the dough into a ball and divide into 4 equal sections. Roll each section into a rope 1 inch thick. Slice the dough into squares with a sharp knife. 4. Preheat the air fryer to

400°F (204°C). 5. Working in batches if necessary, place the gnocchi in a single layer in the basket of the air fryer and spray generously with olive oil. Pausing halfway through the cooking time to turn the gnocchi, air fry for 25 to 30 minutes until golden brown and crispy on the edges. Transfer to a large bowl and toss with the melted butter and Parmesan cheese.

Per Serving:

calories: 220 | fat: 20g | protein: 7g | carbs: 8g | net carbs: 5g | fiber: 3g

Crispy Tofu

Preparation time: 30 minutes | Cook time: 15 to 20 minutes | Serves 4

- ✓ 1 (16-ounce / 454-g) block extra-firm tofu
- ✓ 2 tablespoons coconut aminos
- ✓ 1 tablespoon toasted sesame oil
- ✓ 1 tablespoon olive oil
- ✓ 1 tablespoon chili-garlic sauce
- ✓ 1½ teaspoons black sesame seeds
- ✓ 1 scallion, thinly sliced

Instructions

1. Press the tofu for at least 15 minutes by wrapping it in paper towels and setting a heavy pan on top so that the moisture drains. 2. Slice the tofu into bite-size cubes and transfer to a bowl. Drizzle with the coconut aminos, sesame oil, olive oil, and chili-garlic sauce. Cover and refrigerate for 1 hour or up to overnight. 3. Preheat the air fryer to 400°F (204°C). 4. Arrange the tofu in a single layer in the air fryer basket. Pausing to shake the pan halfway through the cooking time, air fry for 15 to 20 minutes until crisp. Serve with any juices that accumulate in the bottom of the air fryer, sprinkled with the sesame seeds and sliced scallion.

Per Serving:

calories: 186 | fat: 14g | protein: 12g | carbs: 4g | net carbs: 3g | fiber: 1g

CHAPTER 7 Stews and Soups

Salmon and Tomatillos Stew

Preparation time: 15 minutes | Cook time: 12 minutes | Serves 2

- ✓ 10 ounces (283 g) salmon fillet, chopped
- ✓ 2 tomatillos, chopped
- ✓ ½ teaspoon ground turmeric
- ✓ 1 cup coconut cream
- ✓ 1 teaspoon ground paprika
- ✓ ½ teaspoon salt

Instructions

1. Put all ingredients in the Instant Pot. Stir to mix well. 2. Close the lid. Select Manual mode and set cooking time for 12 minutes on Low Pressure. 3. When timer beeps, use a quick pressure release. Open the lid. 4. Serve warm.

Per Serving:

calories: 479 | fat: 38g | protein: 31g | carbs: 10g | net carbs: 6g | fiber: 4g

Broccoli Brie Soup

Preparation time: 5 minutes | Cook time: 14 minutes | Serves 6

- ✓ 1 tablespoon coconut oil or unsalted butter
- ✓ 1 cup finely diced onions
- ✓ 1 head broccoli, cut into small florets
- ✓ 2½ cups chicken broth or vegetable broth
- ✓ 8 ounces (227 g) Brie cheese, cut off rind and cut into chunks
- ✓ 1 cup unsweetened almond milk or heavy cream, plus more for drizzling
- ✓ Fine sea salt and ground black pepper, to taste
- ✓ Extra-virgin olive oil, for drizzling
- ✓ Coarse sea salt, for garnish

Instructions

1. Place the coconut oil in the Instant Pot and press Sauté. Once hot, add the onions and sauté for 4 minutes, or until soft. Press Cancel to stop the Sauté. 2. Add the broccoli and broth. Seal the lid, press Manual, and set the timer for 10 minutes. Once finished, let the pressure release naturally. 3. Remove the lid and add the Brie and almond milk to the pot. Transfer the soup to a food processor or blender and process until smooth, or purée the soup right in the pot with a stick blender. 4. Season with salt and pepper to taste. Ladle the soup into bowls and drizzle with almond milk and olive oil. Garnish with coarse sea salt and freshly ground pepper.

Per Serving:

calories: 210 | fat: 16g | protein: 9g | carbs: 7g | net carbs: 6g | fiber: 1g

Chilled Cilantro and Avocado Soup

Preparation time: 10 minutes | Cook time: 7 minutes | Serves 6

- ✓ 2 to 3 tablespoons olive oil
- ✓ 1 large white onion, diced
- ✓ 3 garlic cloves, crushed
- ✓ 1 serrano chile, seeded and diced
- ✓ Salt and freshly ground black pepper, to taste
- ✓ 4 or 5 ripe avocados, peeled, halved, and pitted
- ✓ 4 cups chicken broth, or vegetable broth
- ✓ 2 cups water
- ✓ Juice of 1 lemon
- ✓ ¼ cup chopped fresh cilantro, plus more for garnish
- ✓ ½ cup sour cream

Instructions

1. In a large pan over medium heat, heat the olive oil. 2. Add the onion and garlic. Sauté for 5 to 7 minutes until the onion is softened and translucent. 3. Add the serrano, season with salt and pepper, and remove from the heat. 4. In a blender, combine the avocados, chicken broth, water, lemon juice, cilantro, and onion-garlic-chile mixture. Purée until smooth (you may have to do this in batches), strain through a fine-mesh sieve, and season with more salt and pepper. Refrigerate, covered, for about 3 hours or until chilled through. 5. To serve, top with sour cream and a sprinkle of chopped cilantro.

Refrigerate leftovers in an airtight container for up to 1 week.

Per Serving:

calories: 513 | fat: 45g | protein: 7g | carbs: 20g | net carbs: 8g | fiber: 12g

Buffalo Chicken Soup

Preparation time: 7 minutes | Cook time: 10 minutes | Serves 2

- ✓ 1 ounce (28 g) celery stalk, chopped
- ✓ 4 tablespoons coconut milk
- ✓ ¾ teaspoon salt
- ✓ ¼ teaspoon white pepper
- ✓ 1 cup water
- ✓ 2 ounces (57 g) Mozzarella, shredded
- ✓ 6 ounces (170 g) cooked chicken, shredded
- ✓ 2 tablespoons keto-friendly Buffalo sauce

Instructions

1. Place the chopped celery stalk, coconut milk, salt, white pepper, water, and Mozzarella in the Instant Pot. Stir to mix well. 2. Set the Manual mode and set timer for 7 minutes on High Pressure. 3. When timer beeps, use a quick pressure release and open the lid. 4. Transfer the soup on the bowls. Stir in the chicken and Buffalo sauce. Serve warm.

Per Serving:

calories: 287 | fat: 15g | protein: 33g | carbs: 4g | net carbs: 3g | fiber: 1g

Cream of Mushroom Soup

Preparation time: 10 minutes | Cook time: 10 minutes | Serves 4

- ✓ 1 pound (454 g) sliced button mushrooms
- ✓ 3 tablespoons butter
- ✓ 2 tablespoons diced onion
- ✓ 2 cloves garlic, minced
- ✓ 2 cups chicken broth
- ✓ ½ teaspoon salt
- ✓ ¼ teaspoon pepper
- ✓ ½ cup heavy cream
- ✓ ¼ teaspoon xanthan gum

Instructions

1. Press the Sauté button and then press the Adjust button to set heat to Less. Add mushrooms, butter, and onion to pot. Sauté for 5 to 8 minutes or until onions and mushrooms begin to brown. Add garlic and sauté until fragrant. Press the Cancel button. 2. Add broth, salt, and pepper. Click lid closed. Press the Manual button and adjust time for 3 minutes. When timer beeps, quick-release the pressure. Stir in heavy cream and xanthan gum. Allow a few minutes to thicken and serve warm.

Per Serving:

calories: 220 | fat: 19g | protein: 5g | carbs: 6g | net carbs: 5g | fiber: 1g

Venison and Tomato Stew

Preparation time: 12 minutes | Cook time: 42 minutes | Serves 8

- ✓ 1 tablespoon unsalted butter
- ✓ 1 cup diced onions
- ✓ 2 cups button mushrooms, sliced in half
- ✓ 2 large stalks celery, cut into ¼-inch pieces
- ✓ Cloves squeezed from 2 heads roasted garlic or 4 cloves garlic, minced
- ✓ 2 pounds (907 g) boneless venison or beef roast, cut into 4 large pieces
- ✓ 5 cups beef broth
- ✓ 1 (14½-ounce / 411-g) can diced tomatoes
- ✓ 1 teaspoon fine sea salt
- ✓ 1 teaspoon ground black pepper
- ✓ ½ teaspoon dried rosemary, or 1 teaspoon fresh rosemary, finely chopped
- ✓ ½ teaspoon dried thyme leaves, or 1 teaspoon fresh thyme leaves, finely chopped
- ✓ ½ head cauliflower, cut into large florets
- ✓ Fresh thyme leaves, for garnish

Instructions

1. Place the butter in the Instant Pot and press Sauté. Once melted, add the onions and sauté for 4 minutes, or until soft. 2. Add the mushrooms, celery, and garlic and sauté for another 3 minutes, or until the mushrooms are golden brown. Press Cancel to stop the Sauté. Add the roast, broth, tomatoes, salt, pepper, rosemary, and thyme. 3. Seal the lid, press Manual, and set the timer for 30 minutes. Once

finished, turn the valve to venting for a quick release. 4. Add the cauliflower. Seal the lid, press Manual, and set the timer for 5 minutes. Once finished, let the pressure release naturally. 5. Remove the lid and shred the meat with two forks. Taste the liquid and add more salt, if needed. Ladle the stew into bowls. Garnish with thyme leaves.

Per Serving:

calories: 359 | fat: 21g | protein: 32g | carbs: 9g | net carbs: 6g | fiber: 3g

Broccoli Cheddar Pancetta Soup

Preparation time: 15 minutes | Cook time: 30 minutes | Serves 6

- ✓ 2 ounces (57 g) pancetta, diced
- ✓ 2 tablespoons butter or ghee
- ✓ ¼ medium onion, finely chopped (about ½ cup)
- ✓ 3 garlic cloves, minced
- ✓ 3 cups bone broth
- ✓ ½ cup heavy (whipping) cream
- ✓ 2 cups broccoli florets, chopped into bite-size pieces
- ✓ 1 teaspoon garlic powder
- ✓ 1 teaspoon onion powder
- ✓ 1 teaspoon paprika
- ✓ 1 teaspoon salt
- ✓ ½ teaspoon freshly ground black pepper
- ✓ Pinch cayenne pepper
- ✓ ½ tablespoon gelatin (or ½ teaspoon xanthan or guar gum), for thickening
- ✓ 2 cups shredded sharp Cheddar cheese

Instructions

1. In a large pot over medium heat, cook the pancetta, stirring often, until crisp. Remove the pancetta pieces to a paper towel using a slotted spoon, leaving as much grease as possible in the pot. 2. Add the butter, onion, and garlic to the pot and sauté for 5 minutes. 3. Add the bone broth, cream, broccoli, garlic, onion, paprika, salt, pepper, and cayenne to the pot and stir well. Sprinkle in the gelatin and stir until well incorporated. Bring to a boil. 4. Once boiling, reduce the heat to low and simmer for 10 to

15 minutes, stirring occasionally. 5. Then, with the heat on low, gradually add the cheese, ½ cup at a time, stirring constantly. Once all of the cheese has been added, remove the pot from the heat. Sprinkle the pancetta pieces over the top and serve. 6. To store, divide the soup into glass jars and freeze for easy meals throughout the coming weeks and months. Make sure to only fill the jars three-quarters full because the liquid will expand as it freezes.

Per Serving:

1½ cups: calories: 311 | fat: 29g | protein: 17g | carbs: 5g | net carbs: 4g | fiber: 1g

Chicken Cauliflower Rice Soup

Preparation time: 5 minutes | Cook time: 20 minutes | Serves 4

- ✓ 4 tablespoons butter
- ✓ ¼ cup diced onion
- ✓ 2 stalks celery, chopped
- ✓ ½ cup fresh spinach
- ✓ ½ teaspoon salt
- ✓ ¼ teaspoon pepper
- ✓ ¼ teaspoon dried thyme
- ✓ ¼ teaspoon dried parsley
- ✓ 1 bay leaf
- ✓ 2 cups chicken broth
- ✓ 2 cups diced cooked chicken
- ✓ ¾ cup uncooked cauliflower rice
- ✓ ½ teaspoon xanthan gum (optional)

Instructions

1. Press the Sauté button and add butter to Instant Pot. Add onions and sauté until translucent. Place celery and spinach into Instant Pot and sauté for 2 to 3 minutes until spinach is wilted. Press the Cancel button. 2. Sprinkle seasoning into Instant Pot and add bay leaf, broth, and cooked chicken. Click lid closed. Press the Soup button and adjust time for 10 minutes. 3. When timer beeps, quick-release the pressure and stir in cauliflower rice. Leave Instant Pot on Keep Warm setting to finish cooking cauliflower rice additional 10 minutes. Serve warm. 4. For a thicker soup, stir in xanthan gum.

Per Serving:

calories: 228 | fat: 14g | protein: 22g | carbs: 3g | net carbs: 2g | fiber: 1g

Beef Chili

Preparation time: 5 minutes | Cook time: 50 minutes | Serves 4

- ✓ ½ green bell pepper, cored, seeded, and chopped
- ✓ ½ medium onion, chopped
- ✓ 2 tablespoons extra-virgin olive oil
- ✓ 1 tablespoon minced garlic
- ✓ 1 pound (454 g) ground beef (80/20)
- ✓ 1 (14-ounce / 397-g) can crushed tomatoes
- ✓ 1 cup beef broth
- ✓ 1 tablespoon ground cumin
- ✓ 1 tablespoon chili powder
- ✓ 2 teaspoons paprika
- ✓ 1 teaspoon pink Himalayan sea salt
- ✓ ¼ teaspoon cayenne pepper

Instructions

1. In a medium pot, combine the bell pepper, onion, and olive oil. Cook over medium heat for 8 to 10 minutes, until the onion is translucent. 2. Add the garlic and cook for 1 minute longer, until fragrant. 3. Add the ground beef and cook for 7 to 10 minutes, until browned. 4. Add the tomatoes, broth, cumin, chili powder, paprika, salt, and cayenne. Stir to combine. 5. Simmer the chili for 30 minutes, until the flavors come together, then enjoy.

Per Serving:

calories: 406 | fat: 31g | protein: 22g | carbs: 12g | net carbs: 8g | fiber: 4g

Beef and Spinach Stew

Preparation time: 20 minutes | Cook time: 30 minutes | Serves 4

- ✓ 1 pound (454 g) beef sirloin, chopped
- ✓ 2 cups spinach, chopped
- ✓ 3 cups chicken broth
- ✓ 1 cup coconut milk
- ✓ 1 teaspoon allspices
- ✓ 1 teaspoon coconut aminos

Instructions

1. Put all ingredients in the Instant Pot. Stir to mix well. 2. Close the lid. Set the Manual mode and set cooking time for 30 minutes on High Pressure. 3. When timer beeps, use a natural pressure release for 10 minutes, then release any remaining pressure. Open the lid. 4. Blend with an immersion blender until smooth. 5. Serve warm.

Per Serving:

calories: 383 | fat: 22g | protein: 40g | carbs: 5g | net carbs: 3g | fiber: 2g

Vegan Pho

Preparation time: 10 minutes | Cook time: 20 minutes | serves 8

- ✓ 8 cups vegetable broth
- ✓ 1-inch knob fresh ginger, peeled and chopped
- ✓ 2 tablespoons tamari
- ✓ 3 cups shredded fresh spinach
- ✓ 2 cups chopped broccoli
- ✓ 1 cup sliced mushrooms
- ✓ ½ cup chopped carrots
- ✓ ⅓ cup chopped scallions
- ✓ 1 (8-ounce) package shirataki noodles
- ✓ 2 cups shredded cabbage
- ✓ 2 cups mung bean sprouts
- ✓ Fresh Thai basil leaves, for garnish
- ✓ Fresh cilantro leaves, for garnish
- ✓ Fresh mint leaves, for garnish
- ✓ 1 lime, cut into 8 wedges, for garnish

Instructions

1. In a large stockpot over medium-high heat, bring the vegetable broth to a simmer with the ginger and tamari. 2. Once the broth is hot, add the spinach, broccoli, mushrooms, carrots, and scallions, and simmer for a few minutes, just until the vegetables start to become tender. 3. Stir in the shirataki noodles, then remove the pot from the heat and divide the soup among serving bowls. 4. Top each bowl with cabbage, sprouts, basil, cilantro, mint, and a lime wedge.

Per Serving:

calories: 47 | fat: 0g | protein: 3g | carbs: 10g | net carbs: 7g | fiber: 3g

Blue Cheese Mushroom Soup

Preparation time: 15 minutes | Cook time: 20 minutes | Serves 4

- ✓ 2 cups chopped white mushrooms
- ✓ 3 tablespoons cream cheese
- ✓ 4 ounces (113 g) scallions, diced
- ✓ 4 cups chicken broth
- ✓ 1 teaspoon olive oil
- ✓ ½ teaspoon ground cumin
- ✓ 1 teaspoon salt
- ✓ 2 ounces (57 g) blue cheese, crumbled

Instructions

1. Combine the mushrooms, cream cheese, scallions, chicken broth, olive oil, and ground cumin in the Instant Pot. 2. Seal the lid. Select Manual mode and set cooking time for 20 minutes on High Pressure. 3. When timer beeps, use a quick pressure release and open the lid. 4. Add the salt and blend the soup with an immersion blender. 5. Ladle the soup in the bowls and top with blue cheese. Serve warm.

Per Serving:

calories: 142 | fat: 9g | protein: 10g | carbs: 5g | net carbs: 4g | fiber: 1g

Bacon Cheddar Cauliflower Soup

Preparation time: 15 minutes | Cook time: 30 minutes | Serves 6

- ✓ 1 large head cauliflower, chopped into florets
- ✓ ¼ cup olive oil
- ✓ Salt and freshly ground black pepper, to taste
- ✓ 12 ounces (340 g) bacon, chopped
- ✓ ½ onion, roughly chopped
- ✓ 2 garlic cloves, minced
- ✓ 2 cups chicken broth, or vegetable broth, plus more as needed
- ✓ 2 cups heavy (whipping) cream, plus more as needed
- ✓ ½ cup shredded Cheddar cheese, plus more for topping
- ✓ Sliced scallion, green parts only, or fresh chives, for garnish

Instructions

1. Preheat the oven to 400°F (205°C). 2. On a large rimmed baking sheet, toss the cauliflower with the olive oil and season with salt and pepper. Bake for 25 to 30 minutes or until slightly browned. 3. While the cauliflower roasts, in a large saucepan over medium heat, cook the bacon for 5 to 7 minutes until crispy. Transfer the bacon to a paper towel-lined plate to drain; leave the bacon fat in the pan. 4. Return the pan to medium heat and add the onion and garlic. Stir well to combine and sauté for 5 to 7 minutes until the onion is softened and translucent. Season with salt and pepper. 5. Remove the cauliflower from the oven and add it to the pan with the onion and garlic. Stir in the broth and bring the liquid to a simmer. Reduce the heat to low. Cook for 5 to 7 minutes. Remove from the heat. With an immersion blender, carefully blend the soup. Alternatively, transfer the soup to a regular blender (working in batches if necessary), blend until smooth, and return the soup to the pan. 6. Stir in the cream. You may need to add a bit more broth or cream, depending on how thick you like your soup. Add the Cheddar and stir until melted and combined. Spoon the soup into bowls and top with bacon and more Cheddar. Garnish with scallion.

Per Serving:

1 cup: calories: 545 | fat: 49g | protein: 15g | carbs: 11g | net carbs: 7g | fiber: 4g

Chicken and Mushroom Soup

Preparation time: 5 minutes | Cook time: 15 minutes | Serves 4

- ✓ 1 onion, cut into thin slices
- ✓ 3 garlic cloves, minced
- ✓ 2 cups chopped mushrooms
- ✓ 1 yellow summer squash, chopped
- ✓ 1 pound (454 g) boneless, skinless chicken breast, cut into large chunks
- ✓ 2½ cups chicken broth
- ✓ 1 teaspoon salt
- ✓ 1 teaspoon freshly ground black pepper
- ✓ 1 teaspoon Italian seasoning or poultry seasoning

✓ 1 cup heavy (whipping) cream

Instructions

1. Put the onion, garlic, mushrooms, squash, chicken, chicken broth, salt, pepper, and Italian seasoning in the inner cooking pot of the Instant Pot. 2. Lock the lid into place. Select Manual and adjust the pressure to High. Cook for 15 minutes. When the cooking is complete, let the pressure release naturally for 10 minutes, then quick-release any remaining pressure. Unlock the lid. 3. Using tongs, transfer the chicken pieces to a bowl and set aside. 4. Tilt the pot slightly. Using an immersion blender, roughly purée the vegetables, leaving a few intact for texture and visual appeal. 5. Shred the chicken and stir it back in to the soup. 6. Add the cream and stir well. Serve.

Per Serving:

calories: 427 | fat: 28g | protein: 31g | carbs: 13g | net carbs: 11g | fiber: 2g

Easy Chili

Preparation time: 10 minutes | Cook time: 35 minutes | Serves 6 to 8

✓ 2 pounds ground beef
✓ 2 tablespoons dried minced onions
✓ 2 teaspoons minced garlic
✓ 1 (15 ounces) can tomato sauce
✓ 1 (14½ ounces) can petite diced tomatoes
✓ 1 cup water
✓ 2 tablespoons chili powder
✓ 1 tablespoon ground cumin
✓ ½ teaspoon salt
✓ ½ teaspoon ground black pepper
✓ Suggested Toppings:
✓ Sour cream
✓ Sliced green onions or chopped white onions
✓ Shredded cheddar cheese

Instructions

1. Cook the ground beef, onions, and garlic in a stockpot over medium heat, crumbling the meat with a large spoon as it cooks, until the meat is browned, about 10 minutes. Drain the fat, if necessary. 2. Add the tomato sauce, tomatoes, water, chili powder, cumin, salt, and pepper to the pot. Bring to a boil, then reduce the heat to low and simmer for 20 minutes to allow the flavors to develop and the chili to thicken slightly. 3. Garnish with the chili topping(s) of your choice and serve. Leftovers can be stored in an airtight container in the refrigerator for up to 5 days.

Per Serving:

calories: 429 | fat: 31g | protein: 27g | carbs: 9g | net carbs: 6g | fiber: 3g

Loaded Fauxtato Soup

Preparation time: 5 minutes | Cook time: 20 minutes | serves 4

✓ 3 tablespoons salted butter
✓ ½ cup chopped white onions
✓ 2 cloves garlic, minced
✓ 1 (16 ounces) bag frozen cauliflower florets
✓ 2 cups vegetable broth
✓ 2 cups shredded sharp cheddar cheese, plus extra for garnish
✓ 1 cup heavy whipping cream
✓ Salt and ground black pepper
✓ 8 slices bacon, cooked and cut into small pieces, for garnish

Instructions

1. Melt the butter in a stockpot over medium heat. Sauté the onions and garlic in the butter until the onions are tender and translucent. 2. Add the cauliflower and broth to the pot. Bring to a gentle boil over high heat, then reduce the heat to maintain a simmer and continue cooking until the cauliflower is tender, stirring occasionally, about 15 minutes. 3. Turn the heat down to the lowest setting and add the cheese and cream to the pot. Stir until the cheese is melted and well combined with the rest of the soup. 4. Season to taste with salt and pepper. Serve garnished with extra cheese and bacon pieces. Leftovers can be stored in an airtight container in the refrigerator for up to 5 days.

Per Serving:

calories: 560 | fat: 45g | protein: 5g | carbs: 9g | net carbs: 6g | fiber: 3g

Cauliflower & Blue Cheese Soup

Preparation time: 15 minutes | Cook time: 20 minutes | Serves 5

- ✓ 2 tablespoons extra-virgin avocado oil
- ✓ 1 small red onion, diced
- ✓ 1 medium celery stalk, sliced
- ✓ 1 medium cauliflower, cut into small florets
- ✓ 2 cups vegetable or chicken stock
- ✓ ¼ cup goat's cream or heavy whipping cream
- ✓ Salt and black pepper, to taste
- ✓ 1 cup crumbled goat's or sheep's blue cheese, such as Roquefort
- ✓ 2 tablespoons chopped fresh chives
- ✓ 5 tablespoons extra-virgin olive oil

Instructions

1. Heat a medium saucepan greased with the avocado oil over medium heat. Sweat the onion and celery for 3 to 5 minutes, until soft and fragrant. Add the cauliflower florets and cook for 5 minutes. Add the vegetable stock and bring to a boil. Cook for about 10 minutes, or until the cauliflower is tender. Remove from the heat and let cool for a few minutes. 2. Add the cream. Use an immersion blender, or pour into a blender, to process until smooth and creamy. Season with salt and pepper to taste. Divide the soup between serving bowls and top with the crumbled blue cheese, chives, and olive oil. To store, let cool and refrigerate in a sealed container for up to 5 days.

Per Serving:

calories: 367 | fat: 31g | protein: 12g | carbs: 11g | net carbs: 8g | fiber: 3g

Coconut Shrimp Saffron Soup

Preparation time: 5 minutes | Cook time: 15 minutes | Serves 4

- ✓ 1 tablespoon coconut oil
- ✓ 1 red bell pepper, chopped
- ✓ 2 teaspoons minced garlic
- ✓ 2 teaspoons grated fresh ginger
- ✓ 4 cups chicken stock
- ✓ 1 (15 ounces) can coconut milk
- ✓ 1 pound shrimp, peeled, deveined, and chopped
- ✓ 1 cup shredded kale
- ✓ Juice of 1 lime
- ✓ ½ cup warm water
- ✓ Pinch saffron threads
- ✓ Sea salt, for seasoning
- ✓ 2 tablespoons chopped fresh cilantro

Instructions

1. Sauté the vegetables. In a large saucepan over medium heat, warm the coconut oil. Add the red pepper, garlic, and ginger and sauté until they've softened, about 5 minutes. 2. Simmer the soup. Add the chicken stock and coconut milk and bring the soup to a boil, then reduce the heat to low and stir in the shrimp, kale, and lime juice. Simmer the soup until the shrimp is cooked through, about 5 minutes. 3. Mix in the saffron. While the soup is simmering, stir the saffron and the warm water together in a small bowl and let it sit for 5 minutes. Stir the saffron mixture into the soup when the shrimp is cooked, and simmer the soup for 3 minutes more. 4. Season and serve. Season with salt. Ladle the soup into bowls, garnish it with the cilantro, and serve it hot. Tip: As mentioned above, there's a reason that saffron is expensive, so if you come across some that is cheap, take a close look to make sure it's the real deal. Take a look at the threads, and if the saffron is a uniform color on the whole strand (instead of having a lighter tip), it is probably not real saffron.

Per Serving:

calories: 504 | fat: 36g | protein: 32g | carbs: 15g | net carbs: 12g | fiber: 3g

Creamy Mushroom Soup

Preparation time: 10 minutes | Cook time: 30 minutes | Serves 4

- ✓ 2 slices bacon, cut into ¼-inch dice
- ✓ 2 tablespoons minced shallots or onions
- ✓ 1 teaspoon minced garlic
- ✓ 1 pound (454 g) button mushrooms, cleaned and quartered or sliced
- ✓ 1 teaspoon dried thyme leaves
- ✓ 2 cups chicken bone broth, homemade or store-bought

- ✓ 1 teaspoon fine sea salt
- ✓ ½ teaspoon freshly ground black pepper
- ✓ 2 large eggs
- ✓ 2 tablespoons lemon juice
- ✓ For Garnish:
- ✓ Fresh thyme leaves
- ✓ MCT oil or extra-virgin olive oil, for drizzling

Instructions

1. Place the diced bacon in a stockpot and sauté over medium heat until crispy, about 3 minutes. Remove the bacon from the pan, but leave the drippings. Add the shallots and garlic to the pan with the drippings and sauté over medium heat for about 3 minutes, until softened and aromatic. 2. Add the mushrooms and dried thyme and sauté over medium heat until the mushrooms are golden brown, about 10 minutes. Add the broth, salt, and pepper and bring to boil. 3. Whisk the eggs and lemon juice in a medium bowl. While whisking, very slowly pour in ½ cup of the hot soup (if you add the hot soup too quickly, the eggs will curdle). Slowly whisk another cup of the hot soup into the egg mixture. 4. Pour the hot egg mixture into the pot while stirring. Add the cooked bacon, then reduce the heat and simmer for 10 minutes, stirring constantly. The soup will thicken slightly as it cooks. Remove from the heat. Garnish with fresh thyme and drizzle with MCT oil before serving. 5. This soup is best served fresh but can be stored in an airtight container in the fridge for up to 3 days. To reheat, place in a saucepan over medium-low heat until warmed, stirring constantly to keep the eggs from curdling.

Per Serving:

calories: 185 | fat: 13g | protein: 11g | carbs: 6g | net carbs: 4g | fiber: 2g

Summer Vegetable Soup

Preparation time: 10 minutes | Cook time: 6 minutes | Serves 6

- ✓ 3 cups finely sliced leeks
- ✓ 6 cups chopped rainbow chard, stems and leaves separated
- ✓ 1 cup chopped celery
- ✓ 2 tablespoons minced garlic, divided
- ✓ 1 teaspoon dried oregano
- ✓ 1 teaspoon salt
- ✓ 2 teaspoons freshly ground black pepper
- ✓ 3 cups chicken broth, plus more as needed
- ✓ 2 cups sliced yellow summer squash, ½-inch slices
- ✓ ¼ cup chopped fresh parsley
- ✓ ¾ cup heavy (whipping) cream
- ✓ 4 to 6 tablespoons grated Parmesan cheese

Instructions

1. Put the leeks, chard, celery, 1 tablespoon of garlic, oregano, salt, pepper, and broth into the inner cooking pot of the Instant Pot. 2. Lock the lid into place. Select Manual and adjust the pressure to High. Cook for 3 minutes. When the cooking is complete, quick-release the pressure. Unlock the lid. 3. Add more broth if needed. 4. Turn the pot to Sauté and adjust the heat to high. Add the yellow squash, parsley, and remaining 1 tablespoon of garlic. 5. Allow the soup to cook for 2 to 3 minutes, or until the squash is softened and cooked through. 6. Stir in the cream and ladle the soup into bowls. Sprinkle with the Parmesan cheese and serve.

Per Serving:

calories: 210 | fat: 14g | protein: 10g | carbs: 12g | net carbs: 8g | fiber: 4g

CHAPTER 8 Treats and Desserts

Peanut Butter Mousse

Preparation time: 10 minutes | Cook time: 0 minutes | Serves 4

- ✓ 1 cup heavy (whipping) cream
- ✓ ¼ cup natural peanut butter
- ✓ 1 teaspoon alcohol-free pure vanilla extract
- ✓ 4 drops liquid stevia

Instructions

1. In a medium bowl, beat together the heavy cream, peanut butter, vanilla, and stevia until firm peaks form, about 5 minutes. 2. Spoon the mousse into 4 bowls and place in the refrigerator to chill for 30 minutes. 3. Serve.

Per Serving:

calories: 280 | fat: 28g | protein: 6g | carbs: 4g | net carbs: 3g | fiber: 1g

Mixed Berry Cobbler

Preparation time: 10 minutes | Cook time: 35 minutes | Serves 4

- ✓ Filling:
- ✓ 2 cups frozen mixed berries
- ✓ 1 tablespoon granulated erythritol
- ✓ ½ teaspoon water
- ✓ ¼ teaspoon freshly squeezed lemon juice
- ✓ ¼ teaspoon vanilla extract
- ✓ Crust:
- ✓ ½ cup coconut flour
- ✓ 2 tablespoons granulated erythritol
- ✓ ½ teaspoon xanthan gum
- ✓ ½ teaspoon baking powder
- ✓ 6 tablespoons butter, cold
- ✓ ¼ cup heavy (whipping) cream
- ✓ Topping:
- ✓ 1 teaspoon granulated erythritol
- ✓ ¼ teaspoon ground cinnamon

Instructions

1. Preheat the oven to 350°F (180°C). 2. To make the filling: In a 9-inch round pie dish, combine the berries, erythritol, water, lemon juice, and vanilla. 3. To make the crust: In a food processor, pulse to combine the coconut flour, erythritol, xanthan gum, and baking powder. 4. Add the butter and cream, and pulse until pea-sized pieces of dough form. Don't overprocess. 5. Form 5 equal balls of dough, then flatten them to between ¼- and ½-inch thickness. 6. Place the dough rounds on the top of the berries so that they are touching, but not overlapping. 7. To make the topping: In a small bowl, combine the erythritol and cinnamon. Sprinkle the mixture over the dough. 8. Bake for 30 to 35 minutes, until the topping is beginning to brown, then let cool for 10 minutes before serving.

Per Serving:

calories: 317 | fat: 25g | protein: 4g | carbs: 19g | net carbs: 12g | fiber: 7g

Chewy Chocolate Chip Cookies

Preparation time: 10 minutes | Cook time: 20 minutes | Makes 16 cookies

- ✓ 1½ cups blanched almond flour
- ✓ ½ cup granular erythritol
- ✓ 1 tablespoon unflavored beef gelatin powder
- ✓ 1 teaspoon baking powder
- ✓ ½ cup (1 stick) unsalted butter, melted but not hot
- ✓ 1 large egg
- ✓ 1 teaspoon vanilla extract
- ✓ ½ cup sugar-free chocolate chips

Instructions

1. Preheat the oven to 350°F and line 2 baking sheets with parchment paper. 2. Put the almond flour, erythritol, gelatin, and baking powder in a medium-sized bowl and whisk using a fork. Set aside. 3. Put the melted butter, egg, and vanilla extract in a large bowl and combine using a hand mixer or whisk. Add the dry mixture to wet mixture in 2 batches and combine until you have a soft dough that can easily be rolled between your hands without sticking. 4.

Fold the chocolate chips into the dough with a rubber spatula. Using a cookie scoop or spoon, scoop 16 even-sized balls of the dough onto the baking sheets, leaving 2 inches of space between them. Using your hand or the spatula, flatten the cookies a little. They will spread slightly in the oven. 5. Bake for 20 minutes, or until golden brown. Allow to cool on the baking sheets for 15 minutes prior to handling. 6. Store leftovers in a sealed container in the refrigerator for up to a week or freeze for up to a month.

Per Serving:

calories: 125 | fat: 12g | protein: 3g | carbs: 3g | net carbs: 1g | fiber: 2g

Keto Cheesecake with Pecan Almond Crust

Preparation time: 20 minutes | Cook time: 1 hour 45 minutes | serves 16

- ✓ Crust:
- ✓ 1 cup finely ground blanched almond flour
- ✓ 1 cup raw pecan halves, finely crushed
- ✓ ½ cup granular erythritol
- ✓ ¼ cup (½ stick) salted butter, cubed
- ✓ Filling:
- ✓ 5 (8 ounces) packages cream cheese, softened
- ✓ 1½ cups confectioners'-style erythritol
- ✓ 4 large eggs
- ✓ 1 cup sour cream
- ✓ 1 tablespoon freshly squeezed lemon juice
- ✓ 1 teaspoon vanilla extract

Make The Crust: Instructions

1. Preheat the oven to 375°F. Grease the bottom and side of a 9- or 10-inch springform pan with butter, or line it with parchment paper cut to fit the bottom of the pan and grease the sides. 2. Place all the crust ingredients in a mixing bowl and mix with a fork until well combined. The mixture will be crumbly. Press the crust mixture into the prepared pan. 3. Par-bake the crust for 12 to 15 minutes, until brown around the edges. 4. Remove the crust from the oven and turn the oven temperature down to 325°F. Let the crust cool completely, then make the filling.

Make The Filling: Instructions

1. Using a hand mixer, beat the cream cheese on medium speed until fluffy. 2. With the mixer still on medium speed, gradually blend in the erythritol. 3. Blend in the eggs one at a time, scraping down the bowl after each addition. 4. Beat in the sour cream, then add the lemon juice and vanilla extract. At this point, the batter will be very thick and creamy. To bake the cheesecake: Instructions

1. Wrap the bottom of the cooled springform pan in aluminum foil (this will protect the cake when it sits in the water bath). 2. Pour the filling over the cooled crust, then set the springform pan inside a roasting pan. 3. Pour hot water into the roasting pan so that it comes halfway up the side of the springform pan. 4. Bake the cheesecake for 1 hour 30 minutes or until the center is firm and the top is slightly browned. 5. Remove the springform pan from the water bath. Let the cheesecake cool completely, then refrigerate for at least 8 hours or overnight. 6. Before serving, run a knife around the rim of the pan to loosen the cake, then release the side of the pan. Leftovers can be stored in an airtight container in the refrigerator for up to 5 days.

Per Serving:

calories: 315 | fat: 28g | protein: 9g | carbs: 4g | net carbs: 2g | fiber: 1g

Strawberry Shortcakes

Preparation time: 10 minutes | Cook time: 15 minutes | serves 6

- ✓ 1½ cups fresh strawberries
- ✓ ¾ cup finely ground blanched almond flour
- ✓ 1 teaspoon baking powder
- ✓ ⅛ teaspoon salt
- ✓ 1 large egg
- ✓ ⅓ cup granular erythritol
- ✓ 2 tablespoons heavy whipping cream
- ✓ 2 tablespoons salted butter, melted but not hot
- ✓ ½ teaspoon vanilla extract
- ✓ 1½ cups whipped cream, for serving

Instructions

1. Preheat the oven to 375°F. Line a baking sheet

with parchment paper. 2. Hull and slice the strawberries and set aside. 3. In a small bowl, whisk together the almond flour, baking powder, and salt. 4. In a medium-sized mixing bowl, whisk the egg, then stir in the erythritol, cream, melted butter, and vanilla extract. While stirring, slowly add the dry ingredients; continue stirring until well blended. 5. Drop spoonfuls of the batter onto the prepared baking sheet, spacing the shortcakes 2 inches apart, to make a total of 6 shortcakes. Bake for 13 to 15 minutes, until the shortcakes are golden brown on the tops and a toothpick or tester inserted in the middle of a shortcake comes out clean. Allow to completely cool on the pan. 6. To serve, top the shortcakes with whipped cream and the sliced strawberries. Leftover shortcakes can be stored in an airtight container in the refrigerator for up to 5 days.

Per Serving:

calories: 154 | fat: 13g | protein: 4g | carbs: 5g | net carbs: 3g | fiber: 2g

Almond Pie with Coconut

Preparation time: 5 minutes | Cook time: 41 minutes | Serves 8

- ✓ 1 cup almond flour
- ✓ ½ cup coconut milk
- ✓ 1 teaspoon vanilla extract
- ✓ 2 tablespoons butter, softened
- ✓ 1 tablespoon Truvia
- ✓ ¼ cup shredded coconut
- ✓ 1 cup water

Instructions

1. In the mixing bowl, mix up almond flour, coconut milk, vanilla extract, butter, Truvia, and shredded coconut. 2. When the mixture is smooth, transfer it in the baking pan and flatten. 3. Pour water and insert the trivet in the instant pot. 4. Put the baking pan with cake on the trivet. 5. Lock the lid. Select the Manual mode and set the cooking time for 41 minutes on High Pressure. Once the timer goes off, perform a natural pressure release for 10 minutes, then release any remaining pressure. Carefully open the lid. 6. Serve immediately.

Per Serving:

calories: 89 | fat: 9g | protein: 1g | carbs: 3g | net carbs: 2g | fiber: 1g

Crustless Cheesecake Bites

Preparation time: 10 minutes | Cook time: 30 minutes | Serves 4

- ✓ 4 ounces cream cheese, at room temperature
- ✓ ¼ cup sour cream
- ✓ 2 large eggs
- ✓ ⅓ cup Swerve natural sweetener
- ✓ ¼ teaspoon vanilla extract

Instructions

1. Preheat the oven to 350°F. 2. In a medium mixing bowl, use a hand mixer to beat the cream cheese, sour cream, eggs, sweetener, and vanilla until well mixed. 3. Place silicone liners (or cupcake paper liners) in the cups of a muffin tin. 4. Pour the cheesecake batter into the liners, and bake for 30 minutes. 5. Refrigerate until completely cooled before serving, about 3 hours. Store extra cheesecake bites in a zip-top bag in the freezer for up to 3 months.

Per Serving:

calories: 169 | fat: 15g | protein: 5g | carbs: 18g | net carbs: 2g | fiber: 0g

Salty Nutty Chocolate Bark

Preparation time: 5 minutes | Cook time: 10 minutes | Makes 20 pieces

- ✓ ½ cup chopped nuts of choice (pecans, pili nuts, macadamia nuts, walnuts, almonds)
- ✓ 8 ounces (227 g) unsweetened 100 percent dark chocolate
- ✓ 2 tablespoons coconut oil, ghee, or butter
- ✓ ½ to 1 teaspoon sweetener of choice, or more
- ✓ ½ teaspoon sea salt

Instructions

1. Preheat the oven to 350°F (180°C). Line a baking sheet with parchment paper or a silicone mat. 2. Spread the nuts on the prepared baking sheet and toast in the oven for 6 to 8 minutes. Remove from the oven and let cool. 3. Meanwhile, in a

microwave-safe dish, mix the chocolate and coconut oil. Microwave in 15-second increments until melted. Add the sweetener and adjust sweetness to your liking. 4. Add the nuts to the chocolate mixture and stir until combined, leaving the parchment paper or silicone mat on the baking sheet. 5. Pour the chocolate mixture onto the baking sheet and spread it out evenly using a spatula. Sprinkle with the sea salt and freeze for 20 to 30 minutes until set. 6. Once set, break the bark into pieces and serve. 7. Store in a resealable plastic bag or airtight container in the freezer.

Per Serving:

calories: 116 | fat: 20g | protein: 2g | carbs: 4g | net carbs: 2g | fiber: 2g

Raspberry Cheesecake

Preparation time: 10 minutes | Cook time: 25 to 30 minutes | Serves 12

- ✓ ⅔ cup coconut oil, melted
- ✓ ½ cup cream cheese, at room temperature
- ✓ 6 eggs
- ✓ 3 tablespoons granulated sweetener
- ✓ 1 teaspoon alcohol-free pure vanilla extract
- ✓ ½ teaspoon baking powder
- ✓ ¾ cup raspberries

Instructions

1. Preheat the oven to 350°F. Line an 8-by-8-inch baking dish with parchment paper and set aside. 2. In a large bowl, beat together the coconut oil and cream cheese until smooth. 3. Beat in the eggs, scraping down the sides of the bowl at least once. 4. Beat in the sweetener, vanilla, and baking powder until smooth. 5. Spoon the batter into the baking dish and use a spatula to smooth out the top. Scatter the raspberries on top. 6. Bake until the center is firm, about 25 to 30 minutes. 7. Allow the cheesecake to cool completely before cutting into 12 squares.

Per Serving:

1 square: calories: 176 | fat: 18g | protein: 6g | carbs: 3g | net carbs: 2g | fiber: 1g

Glazed Coconut Bundt Cake

Preparation time: 30 minutes | Cook time: 55 minutes | serves 10

- ✓ Cake:
- ✓ 2 cups finely ground blanched almond flour
- ✓ ¼ cup coconut flour
- ✓ ¾ cup granular erythritol
- ✓ 2 teaspoons baking powder
- ✓ ½ teaspoon salt
- ✓ 5 large eggs
- ✓ ½ cup (1 stick) salted butter, softened
- ✓ ¼ cup coconut oil, softened
- ✓ 2 teaspoons vanilla extract
- ✓ 1 cup unsweetened coconut flakes
- ✓ Garnish:
- ✓ ½ cup unsweetened coconut flakes
- ✓ Glaze:
- ✓ ½ cup confectioners'-style erythritol
- ✓ ¼ cup heavy whipping cream
- ✓ ¼ teaspoon vanilla extract

Instructions

1. Preheat the oven to 350°F. Grease a 12-cup Bundt pan with butter. 2. In a medium-sized bowl, whisk the almond flour, coconut flour, granular erythritol, baking powder, and salt. In a large mixing bowl, use a hand mixer on low speed to blend the eggs, butter, coconut oil, and vanilla extract. With the mixer on low speed, slowly blend in the flour mixture. Use a spoon to stir in the coconut flakes. 3. Spoon the batter into the prepared pan, then smooth the top. Bake for 45 minutes, until a toothpick or tester inserted into the middle comes out clean. Place the pan on a wire rack to cool completely. Lower the oven temperature to 325°F for toasting the coconut. 4. Make the toasted coconut garnish: Line a sheet pan with parchment paper. Spread the coconut in a thin layer on the prepared pan. Bake for 5 minutes, stir the coconut, then return to the oven and bake until golden brown. It shouldn't take more than another 5 minutes; keep a close eye on it, as coconut can burn quickly. Remove the coconut from the pan and allow to cool. 5. Make the glaze: Put the

confectioners'-style erythritol, cream, and vanilla extract in a small bowl and stir until smooth. 6. To serve, gently loosen the sides of the cooled cake from the pan with a knife and turn it onto a cake plate. Pour the glaze evenly over the cake. Garnish the cake with the toasted coconut. The cake can be kept covered on the counter for a day. Leftovers can be stored in an airtight container in the refrigerator for up to a week.

Per Serving:

calories: 361 | fat: 31g | protein: 10g | carbs: 7g | net carbs: 3g | fiber: 4g

Pumpkin Walnut Cheesecake

Preparation time: 15 minutes | Cook time: 50 minutes | Serves 6

- ✓ 2 cups walnuts
- ✓ 4 tablespoons melted butter
- ✓ 1 teaspoon cinnamon
- ✓ 16 ounces (454 g) cream cheese, softened
- ✓ 1 cup powdered erythritol
- ✓ ⅓ cup heavy cream
- ✓ ⅔ cup pumpkin purée
- ✓ 2 teaspoons pumpkin spice
- ✓ 1 teaspoon vanilla extract
- ✓ 2 eggs
- ✓ 1 cup water

Instructions

1. Preheat oven to 350°F (180°C). Add walnuts, butter, and cinnamon to food processor. Pulse until ball forms. Scrape down sides as necessary. Dough should hold together in ball. 2. Press into greased 7-inch springform pan. Bake for 10 minutes or until it begins to brown. Remove and set aside. While crust is baking, make cheesecake filling. 3. In large bowl, stir cream cheese until completely smooth. Using rubber spatula, mix in erythritol, heavy cream, pumpkin purée, pumpkin spice, and vanilla. 4. In small bowl, whisk eggs. Slowly add them into large bowl, folding gently until just combined. 5. Pour mixture into crust and cover with foil. Pour water into Instant Pot and place steam rack on bottom. Place pan onto steam rack and click lid closed. Press

the Cake button and press the Adjust button to set heat to More. Set timer for 40 minutes. 6. When timer beeps, allow a full natural release. When pressure indicator drops, carefully remove pan and place on counter. Remove foil. Let cool for additional hour and then refrigerate. Serve chilled.

Per Serving:

calories: 578 | fat: 54g | protein: 12g | carbs: 11g | net carbs: 8g | fiber: 3g

Coconut Muffins

Preparation time: 5 minutes | Cook time: 25 minutes | Serves 5

- ✓ ½ cup coconut flour
- ✓ 2 tablespoons cocoa powder
- ✓ 3 tablespoons erythritol
- ✓ 1 teaspoon baking powder
- ✓ 2 tablespoons coconut oil
- ✓ 2 eggs, beaten
- ✓ ½ cup coconut shred

Instructions

1. In the mixing bowl, mix all ingredients. 2. Then pour the mixture into the molds of the muffin and transfer in the air fryer basket. 3. Cook the muffins at 350°F (177°C) for 25 minutes.

Per Serving:

calories: 182 | fat: 14g | protein: 6g | carbs: 12g | net carbs: 5g | fiber: 7g

Lemon-Poppyseed Cookies

Preparation time: 5 minutes | Cook time: 10 minutes | serves 4

- ✓ Nonstick cooking spray
- ✓ 1 cup almond butter
- ✓ ¾ cup monk fruit sweetener
- ✓ 4 tablespoons chia seeds
- ✓ 3 tablespoons fresh grated lemon zest
- ✓ Juice of 1 lemon
- ✓ 1 tablespoon poppy seeds

Instructions

1. Preheat the oven to 350°F. Grease a baking sheet with cooking spray and set aside. 2. In a large mixing bowl, combine the almond butter with the monk

fruit sweetener, chia seeds, lemon zest, lemon juice, and poppy seeds. Mix well, kneading the mixture with your hands. 3. Roll pieces of the dough into cookie-size balls and place them on the prepared baking sheet, spacing them evenly, as some spreading will occur during baking. 4. Bake the cookies for 8 minutes, until golden. 5. Transfer the cookies to a cooling rack. 6. Serve as is or paired with your favorite unsweetened, plant-based milk.

Per Serving:

calories: 460 | fat: 39g | protein: 13g | carbs: 21g | net carbs: 9g | fiber: 12g

Chia and Blackberry Pudding

Preparation time: 5 minutes | Cook time: 0 minutes | Serves 2

- ✓ 1 cup full-fat natural yogurt
- ✓ 2 teaspoons swerve
- ✓ 2 tablespoons chia seeds
- ✓ 1 cup fresh blackberries
- ✓ 1 tablespoon lemon zest
- ✓ Mint leaves, to serve

Instructions

1. Mix together the yogurt and the swerve. Stir in the chia seeds. Reserve 4 blackberries for garnish and mash the remaining ones with a fork until pureed. Stir in the yogurt mixture Chill in the fridge for 30 minutes. When cooled, divide the mixture between 2 glasses. Top each with a couple of blackberries, mint leaves, lemon zest and serve.

Per Serving:

calories: 190 | fat: 8g | protein: 8g | carbs: 23g | net carbs: 9g | fiber: 14g

One-Bowl Butter Cookies

Preparation time: 5 minutes | Cook time: 14 minutes | Makes 12 cookies

- ✓ ½ cup (1 stick) salted butter, softened
- ✓ 1½ cups finely ground blanched almond flour
- ✓ ¼ teaspoon salt
- ✓ ½ cup granular erythritol
- ✓ ½ teaspoon vanilla extract
- ✓ 1 large egg

- ✓ ⅛ teaspoon liquid stevia

Instructions

1. Preheat the oven to 350°F. Line a baking sheet with parchment paper. 2. Put all the ingredients in a medium-sized mixing bowl. Using a hand mixer, slowly blend on low speed, then increase the speed to medium and continue mixing until everything is well combined. 3. Using a small cookie scoop, scoop the dough onto the prepared pan, leaving 2 inches of space between the cookies. Use the back of a fork to press crisscrosses on each cookie. 4. Bake for 12 to 14 minutes, until the cookies start to turn light brown around the edges. Allow to cool completely before removing from the pan. The cookies will continue to firm up as they cool. Leftovers can be stored in an airtight container at room temperature for up to a week.

Per Serving:

calories: 297 | fat: 29g | protein: 3g | carbs: 4g | net carbs: 2g | fiber: 3g

Cholesterol Caring Nut Clusters

Preparation time: 5 minutes | Cook time: 20 minutes | Makes 18 mini clusters

- ✓ Cluster Base:
- ✓ 1 cup macadamia nuts
- ✓ 1 cup pecan halves
- ✓ ½ cup pistachios
- ✓ ¼ cup tahini or coconut butter (although tahini is preferable)
- ✓ 1 large egg
- ✓ 1 teaspoon vanilla powder
- ✓ 2 teaspoons cinnamon
- ✓ Topping:
- ✓ 2 ounces (57 g) dark chocolate
- ✓ 1 tablespoon virgin coconut oil or cacao butter
- ✓ Pinch of flaked salt

Instructions

1. Preheat the oven to 285°F (140°C) fan assisted or 320°F (160°C) conventional. 2. Make the cluster base: Roughly chop the nuts or place in a food processor and pulse until chopped but still chunky. Add the remaining base ingredients. Press the

"dough" into 18 mini muffin cups and bake for 15 to 20 minutes, until crispy. Remove from the oven and allow to cool completely. Just before adding the chocolate topping, place them in the freezer for 5 to 10 minutes. 3. Meanwhile, make the topping: Melt the dark chocolate and coconut oil in a double boiler, or use a heatproof bowl placed over a small saucepan filled with 1 cup of water, placed over medium heat. Let cool to room temperature. Alternatively, use a microwave and melt in short 10- to 15-second bursts until melted, stirring in between. 4. Top the cooled clusters with the melted dark chocolate and flaked salt. Store in a sealed container in the fridge for up to 2 weeks or freeze for up to 3 months.

Per Serving:

calories: 149 | fat: 14g | protein: 3g | carbs: 5g | net carbs: 3g | fiber: 2g

Traditional Kentucky Butter Cake

Preparation time: 5 minutes | Cook time: 35 minutes | Serves 4

- ✓ 2 cups almond flour
- ✓ ¾ cup granulated erythritol
- ✓ 1½ teaspoons baking powder
- ✓ 4 eggs
- ✓ 1 tablespoon vanilla extract
- ✓ ½ cup butter, melted
- ✓ Cooking spray
- ✓ ½ cup water

Instructions

1. In a medium bowl, whisk together the almond flour, erythritol, and baking powder. Whisk well to remove any lumps. 2. Add the eggs and vanilla and whisk until combined. 3. Add the butter and whisk until the batter is mostly smooth and well combined. 4. Grease the pan with cooking spray and pour in the batter. Cover tightly with aluminum foil. 5. Add the water to the pot. Place the Bundt pan on the trivet and carefully lower it into the pot using. 6. Set the lid in place. Select the Manual mode and set the cooking time for 35 minutes on High Pressure. When the timer goes off, do a quick pressure release. Carefully open the lid. 7. Remove the pan from the pot. Let the cake cool in the pan before flipping out onto a plate.

Per Serving:

calories: 179 | fat: 16g | protein: 2g | carbs: 2g | net carbs: 2g | fiber: 0g

Strawberry Cheesecake Mousse

Preparation time: 10 minutes | Cook time: 0 minutes | Serves 2

- ✓ 4 ounces cream cheese, at room temperature
- ✓ 1 tablespoon heavy (whipping) cream
- ✓ 1 teaspoon Swerve natural sweetener or 1 drop liquid stevia
- ✓ 1 teaspoon vanilla extract
- ✓ 4 strawberries, sliced (fresh or frozen)

Instructions

1. Break up the cream cheese block into smaller pieces and distribute evenly in a food processor (or blender). Add the cream, sweetener, and vanilla. 2. Mix together on high. I usually stop and stir twice and scrape down the sides of the bowl with a small rubber scraper to make sure everything is mixed well. 3. Add the strawberries to the food processor, and mix until combined. 4. Divide the strawberry cheesecake mixture between two small dishes, and chill for 1 hour before serving.

Per Serving:

calories: 221 | fat: 21g | protein: 4g | carbs: 11g | net carbs: 4g | fiber: 1g

Fast Chocolate Mousse

Preparation time: 10 minutes | Cook time: 4 minutes | Serves 1

- ✓ 1 egg yolk
- ✓ 1 teaspoon erythritol
- ✓ 1 teaspoon cocoa powder
- ✓ 2 tablespoons coconut milk
- ✓ 1 tablespoon cream cheese
- ✓ 1 cup water, for cooking

Instructions

1. Pour water and insert the steamer rack in the instant pot. 2. Then whisk the egg yolk with erythritol. 3. When the mixture turns into lemon color, add coconut milk, cream cheese, and cocoa

powder. Whisk the mixture until smooth. 4. Then pour it in the glass jar and place it on the steamer rack. 5. Close and seal the lid. 6. Cook the dessert on Manual (High Pressure) for 4 minutes. Make a quick pressure release.

Per Serving:

calories: 162 | fat: 15g | protein: 4g | carbs: 3g | net carbs: 2g | fiber: 1g

Cinnamon Churros

Preparation time: 25 minutes | Cook time: 30 minutes | Serves 12

✓ Churros
✓ ⅔ cup unblanched almond flour
✓ ¼ cup coconut flour
✓ 1 tablespoon flaxseed meal
✓ 1 teaspoon xanthan gum
✓ 1 cup water
✓ ¼ cup unsalted butter
✓ 2 tablespoons 0g net carb sweetener
✓ ¼ teaspoon salt
✓ 2 large eggs, lightly beaten
✓ 1 teaspoon pure vanilla extract
✓ Garnish
✓ 1 tablespoon unsalted butter, melted
✓ 2 teaspoons ground cinnamon
✓ ¼ cup 0g net carb sweetener

Instructions

1. Preheat oven to 350°F. Line a large baking sheet with parchment paper. 2. In a medium bowl, whisk together almond flour, coconut flour, flaxseed meal, and xanthan gum. 3. In a medium pot over medium heat, heat water almost to a boil and mix in ¼ cup butter, 2 tablespoons sweetener, and ¼ teaspoon salt until butter is melted and well blended. Add flour mix and keep stirring until a ball is formed. 4. Return dough to bowl and let cool for 5 minutes. Mix eggs and vanilla in with dough. 5. Let dough cool to room temperature, 10 to 15 minutes. Transfer dough into a pastry piping bag with star tip. Make twelve churros and place on baking sheet. 6. Bake 15 to 20 minutes until deep golden. 7. Remove from oven and brush with butter. Garnish with cinnamon and

sweetener. Serve warm.

Per Serving:

calories: 100 | fat: 9g | protein: 3g | carbs: 6g | net carbs: 2g | fiber: 4g

Double Chocolate Brownies

Preparation time: 5 minutes | Cook time: 15 to 20 minutes | Serves 8

✓ 1 cup almond flour
✓ ½ cup unsweetened cocoa powder
✓ ½ teaspoon baking powder
✓ ⅓ cup Swerve
✓ ¼ teaspoon salt
✓ ½ cup unsalted butter, melted and cooled
✓ 3 eggs
✓ 1 teaspoon vanilla extract
✓ 2 tablespoons mini semisweet chocolate chips

Instructions

1. Preheat the air fryer to 350°F (177°C). Line a cake pan with parchment paper and brush with oil. 2. In a large bowl, combine the almond flour, cocoa powder, baking powder, Swerve, and salt. Add the butter, eggs, and vanilla. Stir until thoroughly combined. (The batter will be thick.) Spread the batter into the prepared pan and scatter the chocolate chips on top. 3. Air fry for 15 to 20 minutes until the edges are set. (The center should still appear slightly undercooked.) Let cool completely before slicing. To store, cover and refrigerate the brownies for up to 3 days.

Per Serving:

calories: 191 | fat: 17g | protein: 6g | carbs: 7g | net carbs: 3g | fiber: 4g

Lemon Cream "Froyo" Bites

Preparation time: 5 minutes | Cook time: 0 minutes | Makes 8 bites

✓ 4 ounces (113 g) cream cheese
✓ 1 teaspoon vanilla extract
✓ ⅓ cup heavy cream
✓ 1½ teaspoons stevia powder
✓ 1 teaspoon grated lemon zest
✓ 2 teaspoons fresh lemon juice

Instructions

1. Blend all the ingredients in a food processor until smooth. Pour the mixture into a silicone mini muffin pan or ice cube tray, or use mini tart cups. (Alternatively, line a small rectangular loaf pan with parchment paper and pour in entire mixture.) 2. Freeze until set. Pop out the individual bites and store in an airtight container in the freezer. Remove from the freezer a few minutes before eating.

Per Serving:

calories: 84 | fat: 8g | protein: 1g | carbs: 1g | net carbs: 1g | fiber: 0g

Lemon Berry Cream Pops

Preparation time: 10 minutes | Cook time: 5 minutes | Makes 8 ice pops

- ✓ Cream Pops:
- ✓ 2 cups coconut cream
- ✓ 1 tablespoon unsweetened vanilla extract
- ✓ Optional: low-carb sweetener, to taste
- ✓ 2 cups raspberries, fresh or frozen and defrosted
- ✓ Coating:
- ✓ 1⅓ cups coconut butter
- ✓ ¼ cup virgin coconut oil
- ✓ Zest from 2 lemons, about 2 tablespoons
- ✓ 1 teaspoon unsweetened vanilla extract

Instructions

1. To make the cream pops: In a bowl, whisk the coconut cream with the vanilla and optional sweetener until smooth and creamy. In another bowl, crush the raspberries using a fork, then add them to the bowl with the coconut cream and mix to combine. 2. Divide the mixture among eight ⅓-cup ice pop molds. Freeze until solid for 3 hours, or until set. 3. To easily remove the ice pops from the molds, fill a pot as tall as the ice pops with warm (not hot) water and dip the ice pop molds in for 15 to 20 seconds. Remove the ice pops from the molds and then freeze again. 4. Meanwhile, prepare the coating: Place the coconut butter and coconut oil in a small saucepan over low heat. Stir until smooth, remove from the heat, and add the lemon zest and vanilla. Let cool to room temperature. 5. Remove the ice pops from the

freezer, two at a time, and, holding the ice pops over the saucepan, use a spoon to drizzle the coating all over. Return to the freezer until fully set, about 10 minutes. Store in the freezer in a resealable bag for up to 3 months.

Per Serving:

calories: 533 | fat: 54g | protein: 3g | carbs: 13g | net carbs: 9g | fiber: 4g

Chocolate-Covered Coffee Bites

Preparation time: 10 minutes | Cook time: 0 minutes | Serves 8

- ✓ Bites:
- ✓ ¼ cup plus 2 tablespoons (90 g) cacao butter
- ✓ ½ cup (75 g) macadamia nuts, roasted
- ✓ 1 tablespoon confectioners'-style erythritol or 1 or 2 drops liquid stevia ½ teaspoon instant coffee (medium or light roast, regular or decaf)
- ✓ 2 tablespoons collagen peptides
- ✓ Chocolate Topping:
- ✓ ¼ cup (56 g) stevia-sweetened chocolate chips, melted
- ✓ Garnish:
- ✓ About ¼ teaspoon large flake sea salt
- ✓ Special Equipment:
- ✓ Silicone mold with eight 1-ounce (30-ml) semispherical cavities

Instructions

1. Place the cacao butter, macadamia nuts, erythritol, and instant coffee in a high-powered blender or food processor. Blend on high speed until the nuts have broken down quite a bit but are still chunky, about 20 seconds. 2. Add the collagen and pulse to combine. 3. Using a spoon, scoop and press the mixture into 8 cavities of a silicone mold. Place the mold in the fridge for 2 hours or in the freezer for 1 hour, until the bites are set. 4. Meanwhile, line a baking sheet with parchment paper or a silicone baking mat and set aside. 5. Remove the mold from the fridge or freezer and pop out the bites onto the prepared baking sheet. Drizzle the melted chocolate over the top, then sprinkle each bite with a pinch of salt. Return the bites to the fridge until the chocolate

is set, about 10 minutes. Enjoy!

Per Serving:

calories: 213 | fat: 20g | protein: 4g | carbs: 4g | net carbs: 2g | fiber: 2g

Cocoa Cookies

Preparation time: 15 minutes | Cook time: 25 minutes | Serves 4

- ✓ ½ cup coconut flour
- ✓ 3 tablespoons cream cheese
- ✓ 1 teaspoon cocoa powder
- ✓ 1 tablespoon erythritol
- ✓ ¼ teaspoon baking powder
- ✓ 1 teaspoon apple cider vinegar
- ✓ 1 tablespoon butter
- ✓ 1 cup water, for cooking

Instructions

1. Make the dough: Mix up coconut flour, cream cheese, cocoa powder, erythritol, baking powder, apple cider vinegar, and butter. Knead the dough, 2. Then transfer the dough in the baking pan and flatten it in the shape of a cookie. 3. Pour water and insert the steamer rack in the instant pot. 4. Put the pan with a cookie in the instant pot. Close and seal the lid. 5. Cook the cookie on Manual (High Pressure) for 25 minutes. Make a quick pressure release. Cool the cookie well.

Per Serving:

calories: 113 | fat: 7g | protein: 2g | carbs: 14g | net carbs: 8g | fiber: 6g

Vanilla Cookies with Hazelnuts

Preparation time: 20 minutes | Cook time: 10 minutes | Serves 6

- ✓ 1 cup almond flour
- ✓ ½ cup coconut flour
- ✓ 1 teaspoon baking soda
- ✓ 1 teaspoon fine sea salt
- ✓ 1 stick butter
- ✓ 1 cup Swerve
- ✓ 2 teaspoons vanilla
- ✓ 2 eggs, at room temperature
- ✓ 1 cup hazelnuts, coarsely chopped

Instructions

1. Preheat the air fryer to 350ºF (177ºC). 2. Mix the flour with the baking soda, and sea salt. 3. In the bowl of an electric mixer, beat the butter, Swerve, and vanilla until creamy. Fold in the eggs, one at a time, and mix until well combined. 4. Slowly and gradually, stir in the flour mixture. Finally, fold in the coarsely chopped hazelnuts. 5. Divide the dough into small balls using a large cookie scoop; drop onto the prepared cookie sheets. Bake for 10 minutes or until golden brown, rotating the pan once or twice through the cooking time. 6. Work in batches and cool for a couple of minutes before removing to wire racks. Enjoy!

Per Serving:

calories: 576 | fat: 50g | protein: 12g | carbs: 26g | net carbs: 7g | fiber: 19g

Appendix 1: 30 Days Meal Plan

DAYS	BREAKFAST	LUNCH	DINNER	SNACK/DESSERT
1	Mushroom Frittata	Chicken Paillard	Butter Chicken	Hushpuppies
2	Lemon-Blueberry Muffins	Turkey Breast Salad	Lemon Garlic Chicken	Devilish Eggs
3	Almond Flour Pancakes	Chicken Florentine	Zesty Grilled Chicken	Chinese Spare Ribs
4	Coffee Smoothie	Cheese Stuffed Chicken	Sausage-Stuffed Peppers	Pimento Cheese
5	Mini Spinach Quiche	French Garlic Chicken	Sweet Beef Curry	Baked Crab Dip
6	Egg-Stuffed Avocados	Coconut Chicken	Spinach Feta Stuffed Pork	Lime Brussels Chips
7	Flappa Jacks	Balsamic Turkey Thighs	Deconstructed Egg Rolls	Cookie Fat Bombs
8	Chicken and Egg Sandwich	Ham Chicken with Cheese	Beef Shami Kabob	Warm Herbed Olives
9	Glazed Chocolate Donuts	Quattro Formaggi Chicken	Barbacoa Beef Roast	Keto Taco Shells
10	Meat Waffles/Bagels	Butter and Bacon Chicken	Garlic Balsamic London Broil	Taco Beef Bites
11	Bacon Egg Cups	Shredded Chicken	Mississippi Pot Roast	Garlic Herb Butter
12	Spinach and Cheese Frittata	Turmeric Chicken Nuggets	Steak with Bell Pepper	Cauliflower Patties
13	Savory Zucchini Cheddar Waffles	Buffalo Chicken Wings	Zucchini Rolls	Herbed Mushrooms
14	Bacon and Spinach Eggs	Curry Chicken Salad	Pork Meatballs	Garlic Meatballs
15	Blueberry Mug Muffin	Five-Spice Pork Belly	Beef Bourguignon	Cheddar Chips
16	Blackberry Vanilla	Chili-Stuffed	Grilled Herbed Pork	Almond Pie with

	Cake	Avocados	Kebabs	Coconut
17	Bacon-Artichoke Omelet	Parmesan-Crusted Salmon	Beef and Red Cabbage Stew	Crustless Cheesecake Bites
18	Keto Quiche	Cod Fillet with Olives	Pork Taco Casserole	Salty Nutty Chocolate Bark
19	Lettuce Wrapped Chicken Sandwich	Coconut Crab Patties	Pork in White Wine	Raspberry Cheesecake
20	Cheesy Bell Pepper Eggs	Coconut Curry Mussels	Beef Zucchini Boats	Glazed Coconut Bundt Cake
21	Pumpkin Coconut Flour Pancakes	Chili and Turmeric Haddock	Rainbow Salmon Kebabs	Pumpkin Walnut Cheesecake
22	Almond and Vanilla Pancakes	South Indian Fried Fish	Cod with Parsley Pistou	Coconut Muffins
23	Bacon Cheddar Bites	Cajun Salmon	Dill Salmon Cakes	Lemon-Poppyseed Cookies
24	Protein Waffles	Salmon Oscar	Coconut Shrimp Curry	Chia and Blackberry Pudding
25	Eggs Benedict	Halibut Curry	Shrimp Ceviche Salad	One-Bowl Butter Cookies
26	Quickly Blue Cheese Omelet	Aromatic Monkfish Stew	Grilled Calamari	Strawberry Cheesecake Mousse
27	Easy Skillet Pancakes	Sardine Fritter Wraps	Blackened Salmon	Fast Chocolate Mousse
28	Parmesan Baked Eggs	Ginger Cod	Roasted Garlic Bulbs	Cinnamon Churros
29	Avocado and Eggs	Mascarpone Pork Chops	Pizza Bites	Double Chocolate Brownies
30	Cinnamon Rolls	Shrimp Stuffed Zucchini	Bacon Ranch Dip	Lemon Berry Cream Pops

Appendix 2: Measurement Conversion Chart

Volume Equivalents (Dry):	Temperature Equivalents:
1/8 teaspoon = 0.5 mL	225°F = 107°C
1/4 teaspoon = 1 mL	250°F = 121°C
1/2 teaspoon = 2 mL	275°F = 135°C
3/4 teaspoon = 4 mL	300°F = 149°C
1 teaspoon = 5 mL	325°F = 163°C
1 tablespoon = 15 mL	350°F = 177°C
1/4 cup = 59 mL	375°F = 191°C
1/2 cup = 118 mL	400°F = 204°C
3/4 cup = 177 mL	425°F = 218°C
1 cup = 235 mL	450°F = 232°C
2 cups (or 1 pint) = 475 mL	475°F = 246°C
4 cups (or 1 quart) = 1 L	500°F = 260°C

Weight Equivalents:	Volume Equivalents (Liquid):
1 ounce = 28 g	1/4 cup = 60 mL = 2 fl oz
2 ounces = 57 g	1/2 cup = 120 mL = 4 fl oz
5 ounces = 142 g	1 cup = 240 mL = 8 fl oz
10 ounces = 284 g	2 cups (or 1 pint) = 475 mL = 16 fl oz
15 ounces = 425 g	4 cups (or 1 quart) = 1 L = 32 fl oz
16 ounces (1 pound) = 455 g	1 gallon = 4 L = 128 fl oz
1.5 pounds = 680 g	
2 pounds = 907 g	

Appendix 3: Recipe Index

Made in United States
Troutdale, OR
10/08/2024

23501865R00058